W9-CCV-424

# Handmade in England

## THE TRADITION OF BRITISH CRAFTSMEN

# BOOKS BY SIGMUND A. LAVINE

Handmade in England

Handmade in America

Famous American Architects

Famous Merchants

Famous Industrialists

Kettering: Master Inventor

Steinmetz, Maker of Lightning

Allan Pinkerton, America's First Private Eye

Wonders of the Anthill

Wonders of the Hive

Wonders of the Wasp's Nest

Wonders of the Beetle World

Wonders of the Spider World

Wonders of Animal Disguises

Wonders of Animal Architecture

Strange Partners

Strange Travelers

Water Since the World Began, *with Mart Casey*

# Handmade in England

## THE TRADITION OF BRITISH CRAFTSMEN

*by Sigmund A. Lavine*

ILLUSTRATED WITH PHOTOGRAPHS

DODD, MEAD & COMPANY · NEW YORK

## PICTURE CREDITS

Photographs courtesy of:

Asprey & Company, London, England, 133

Biggs of Maidenhead, England, 2, 12 (right), 14 (top), 15 (left), 31 (right), 33, 34 (bottom), 35, 37 (left), 51 (bottom left), 103, 105 (right), 108 (center), 109 (bottom left and right)

British Information Service, 68 (right)

Christie, Manson, Woods, Ltd., London, England, 7 (top), 11, 12 (left), 14 (bottom), 15 (right), 17 (right), 19, 20, 21, 22, 23 (right), 25, 26 (top left and bottom right), 29, 31 (left), 32, 37 (right), 51 (top), 55, 57 (left), 72 (center), 78, 81 (left), 82, 83, 85, 86 (left), 87, 89, 91 (right), 94 (right), 98 (bottom left), 101, 102 (left), 108 (left and right, 111 (left), 113, 115 (left), 117, 119 (bottom left), 120 (bottom left and right), 125, 132 (top)

Corning Museum of Glass, Corning, New York, 41, 43, 45, 46, 49, 51 (bottom right), 52, 56, 57 (right) 59, 60, 61, 64

Garrard & Company, Crown Jewelers, London, England, 102 (right), 111 (right), 112, 115 (right), 116, 118, 119 (top and bottom right), 120 (top right), 121, 129, 131 (bottom), 132 (bottom)

Gregory & Company, Ltd., London, England, 26 (bottom left), 54 (bottom), 58, 84, 98 (top)

The Metropolitan Museum of Art,
  Bequest of Alfred Duane Pell, 1925, 122
  Cloisters Collection, 1955, 105 (left)
  Morris Loeb Gift, 1956, 26 (right top)
  Rogers Fund, 1909, 4 (right); Rogers Fund, 1914, 90 (right); Rogers Fund, 1932, 13; Rogers Fund, 1937, 72 (left); Rogers Fund, 1952, 67 (left)

The Metropolitan Museum of Art, Gift of:
  Mrs. Russell Sage, 1909, 4 (left)
  Sir Joseph Duveen, 1921, 5
  Mrs. Leonard A. Cohn, 1951, 7 (bottom)
  Mrs. Paul Moore, 1938, 8
  Countess Mona Bismark, 1958, 9
  Mrs. Russell S. Carter, 1938, 67 (right), 71 (left); 1944, 76 (top); 1945, 81 (right)
  Frank Stoner, 1930, 71 (right)
  Mrs. J. Insley Blair, 1933, 72 (right)
  R. Thornton Wilson, 1937, 79 (left); R. Thornton Wilson, 1943, in memory of Florence Ellsworth Wilson, 96 (left)
  Mr. and Mrs. Sigmund J. Katz, 1952, 79 (right)
  The Estate of Anna Moore Romaine, 1921, through Benjamin F. Romaine, Ralph B. Romaine, and Joseph Lentelhon, 94 (left)
  J. Pierpont Morgan, 1917, 103
  Mrs. S. P. Avery, 1897, 109 (center), 126

Parke-Bernet Galleries, New York, New York, 28, 30, 107, 128, 131 (top)

Stair and Company, Inc., New York, New York, facing 1, 17 (left), 23 (left), 24, 34 (top), 54 (top)

Josiah Wedgwood & Sons, Ltd., England, 91 (left), 93

Weiner's Antique Shop, Boston, Massachusetts, 62, 63, 68 (left), 73, 75, 76 (bottom), 86 (right), 88, 90 (left), 92, 96 (right), 98 (bottom right), 127

Copyright © 1968 by Sigmund A. Lavine
All rights reserved
No part of this book may be reproduced in any form
without permission in writing from the publisher
Library of Congress Catalog Card Number: 68-16179
Printed in the United States of America

*For Paul Weiner:*

WHOSE SHOP CONTAINS SO MUCH I CAN'T AFFORD
AND WHOSE FRIENDSHIP IS BEYOND PRICE

# *Acknowledgments*

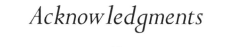

Unlike the master craftsmen of yesteryear who zealously guarded their knowledge and shared it only with those apprenticed to them, antique dealers, collectors, and museum curators of today graciously give all who have an interest in those relics that link the past to the present the benefit of their experience. As a result, the list of individuals who have admitted me to "freedom" on both sides of the Atlantic is a long one. I am indebted to all of them.

However, I would be a most ungrateful "apprentice" if I did not particularly thank E. R. Asprey, managing director of Asprey & Company, London, England; E. T. Biggs, Biggs & Sons, Maidenhead, England; Garrard, Crown Jewelers, London, England; Derek Halfpenny, Wedgwood & Sons, Stoke-on-Trent, England; Jane Lanahan, register of the Corning Museum of Glass, Corning, New York; Linda Rosenkrantz, publicity department, Parke-Bernet Galleries, New York City; M. Arline Lanphear, Stair and Company, New York City; J. A. Vagg, Bracher & Sydenham, Reading, England; R. Melvin-Warner, Gregory & Company, London, England; Paul Weiner, Weiner's Antique Shop, Boston, Massachusetts; D. Welby, London, England; William Young, Aberdeen, Scotland; and the library staff of the Boston Museum of Fine Arts.

Finally, I must express my appreciation to an institution and an individual. The institution is the Milton, Massachusetts, Public Library; the individual, Rosemary Casey of Dodd, Mead & Company. As usual, the librarians of Milton have served me as research assistants, while Rosemary Casey has not only checked my facts, but also assumed the task of preparing my manuscript for publication.

# Contents

# Handmade in England

## THE TRADITION OF BRITISH CRAFTSMEN

# Introduction

————————➤·⁛➌⁛·◄————————

Long before the eighth century when the Venerable Bede taught a group of monks to illuminate manuscripts—an event considered to mark the beginnings of English art—craftsmen were working in England. For example, not all the tin mined in Cornwall was exchanged for the wares carried by the Phoenicians—native smiths fashioned much of it into bronze. Similarly, other artisans created crude benches, blew glass, and molded pottery.

During the Germanic invasions and the Roman occupation, English craftsmen improved their skills by blending native techniques with new methods learned from their foes. Actually, British artisans never stopped borrowing from others, but, while they came under the influence of both Continental and Oriental craftsmen, the articles they fashioned were always unmistakably English in conception.

Eventually, individuals engaged in the same craft banded together. The rules and regulations by which they governed themselves had a dual purpose —they protected the craftsman from the competition of poorly trained hand workers and guaranteed the public that the wares purchased from guild members were of the highest quality. With the founding of the guilds in medieval times the task of tracing the heritage of English craftsmanship becomes easier. There is a mine of information in the records of the various Companies which guarded the rights and enforced the duties of their members—master craftsmen all.

Guild ledgers and other sources of data dealing with British hand workers are familiar to the expert who, like Bunthorne in *Patience*, is

> . . . a judge of blue-and-white and other kinds of pottery—
> From early Oriental down to modern terra-cotta-ry. . . .

But the novice in the antique shop and auction gallery does not know where

*The crafts of furniture, glass, and pottery making are well represented by this display in the Adam style.*

I

to find the basic factual material he desires. Nor does the beginning collector often understand why two different items made by the same craftsman vary in price. The aim of these pages is to supply this information and, in the process, give guidance for further study of English handicraft.

No single volume could, even by generalization and oversimplification, treat all English crafts adequately. Therefore, this book is limited to the story of some of the outstanding men and women who designed pottery and porcelain, blew glass, fashioned silver into utilitarian and beautiful objects, and made furniture. At that, much has had to be omitted. But the advanced collector knows that there are shelves of books dealing with English crafts and dozens of biographies of individual craftsmen.

As a matter of fact, it would be exceedingly brash for anyone to confine the life stories of certain of the greatest creative artists who ever lived, discuss the aesthetic principles that dominated them, describe the social and political climate in which they worked, and evaluate their contributions to English craftsmanship in a single small book. However, it is hoped that the reader will find that "In all ages there have been excellent workmen, and some excellent work done."

*A silver salver in the plain style fashionable in the early Georgian Period.*

# I

## *Furniture*

———————◆※◆———————

Carpentry—one of the oldest of crafts—originated when man began to till the soil and raise animals for food instead of seeking game. Using hand-forged tools, primitive man not only built permanent shelters but also made crude household furnishings Gradually, the making of furniture became a specialized craft, and, while master artisans have worked in wood in all nations, few have displayed the creativeness of the English craftsmen of the seventeenth and eighteenth centuries.

During this period British cabinetmakers developed several of the techniques still employed wherever fine furniture is hand-fashioned and supplied their customers with pieces combining beauty and utility. As a result, their work in the style now known as Queen Anne, Georgian, and Regency set a standard of excellence that contemporary cabinetmakers as well as mass producers of furniture strive to achieve.

Unfortunately, little is known about the majority of the artisans who worked in wood in England before and during this "Golden Age of Furniture." In many cases our only knowledge of early craftsmen is a line or two in an estate account book or a legal document. For example, the census taken of aliens residing in England in 1571 contains the following: "Cornelius Byons, Levina his wif, bothe borne in Flaunders, haue byne here viij moncthes, came to seke lyvinge, beinge a chairemaker, and dwelleth within Matyn de Cinster."

Actually, there is almost as great a lack of information about the makers of furniture now treasured by museums and collectors as there is about such minor craftsmen as Byons. In fact, although certain English cabinetmakers supplied the Crown with furnishings, associated with famous architects, and made their names known to fashionable London through constant newspaper advertising, only the outline of their careers can be seen through the mist of legend. This is true even of Chippendale, Hepplewhite, and Sheraton, whose names are synonymous with recognized styles of furniture.

However, long before the era of Chippendale, Hepplewhite, Sheraton,

3

and their contemporaries—many of whom were their equals—skilled wood-workers were supplying Englishmen with articles designed to meet both social and physical needs. As early as the fourteenth century these craftsmen had banded together in guilds in order to establish standards that would protect both the artisan and the public.

Each guild was jealous of the rights granted it by custom and the charter received from the Crown. Therefore the joiners, who had a monopoly on the making of cupboards, boxes, bedsteads that contained no nails, and "chayres and stooles" held together by the mortise and tenon joint, were constantly bickering with the carpenters. Finally, in 1632, the joiners won two major victories: carpenters were forbidden to fashion any article made with "mortesses and tennants, duftailed, pynned or glued"; and the Aldermen of London ruled that joinery and turning were two distinct crafts.

Turning, the art of shaping wood by lathes, chisels, and gouges, may have been introduced into England by the Romans. But while the origins of the crafts have been lost, it has been established that turners were fashioning chairs in medieval times. The similarity of the turner's use of a lathe from which he formed chair parts and the potter's technique of "throwing" clay on a rapidly revolving wheel is the source of the term applied to chairs made by turners. They are known as "thrown" chairs.

Although the original records of the Turners' Company of London were destroyed in the Great Fire of 1666, its known activities provide an illustra-

LEFT: *Wainscot armchair made about 1600 by joiners.* RIGHT: *Three-legged "thrown" chair made about 1600 by turners using a lathe.*

*An oak chest of the late 14th century.*

tion of guild self-regulation. Not only were turners forbidden to work in joiners' shops, but also a turner had to serve an apprenticeship before qualifying as a journeyman. Then, he had to prove he had mastered his craft by fashioning an article and submitting it to the inspection of a committee of guild members. Among the "masterpieces" of which we have a record are the high chair made by Richard Freeman in 1609 and the woman's stool turned by Ambrose Busher in 1612.

Besides supervising the production of its members, the Turners' Company had the right of inspection and authority to evaluate the "thrown" chairs of unregistered craftsmen as well as those shipped into London for sale. Such chairs were taken to Turners' Hall for examination. If painted—the fashion of painting furniture in England dates from the twelfth century when medieval craftsmen decorated chests and wall cupboards with tempera—an inspection fee of six shillings a dozen was charged. Unpainted chairs cost their makers a fee of seven shillings a dozen—the higher rate probably being established to discourage competition.

Guild representatives gave chairs submitted for approval careful scrutiny. In 1609, upon discovering that a shipment of chairs from Colchester had poplar seats, the Turners' Company advised the maker that he had two choices: either replace the poplar with oak or take the chairs out of London. If he did neither, they threatened to destroy the chairs.

While the cottages of serfs in feudal England were almost bare of household furnishings, the great castles did contain a few stools, benches attached to the walls, and receptacles built into the walls or formed by a curtained or doored alcove.

The most important article of medieval furniture was the chest. Usually these were massive pieces made by joiners who often ornamented their work with chip carving. This geometric decoration requires far less skill than freehand relief carving because the pattern is formed by a compass.

Small chests were also made during this period, including those fashioned of leather. These chests, known technically as coffers, were used to transport clothing and valuables. They were made by coffer makers (the first reference to these craftsmen is in 1373) who, in 1517, merged with the Leathersellers' Company. Incidently, certain coffer makers also covered chairs with leather. The Greene family, for example, performed this service for the Crown from the reign of Henry VIII through that of James I.

Actually, chairs were as rare in medieval England as a warm castle on a winter's night. While a lord might sit in his Great Hall in a thronelike oak chair—which was too heavy to move—and his wife might sit in a smaller one, vassals and guests had to be satisfied with stools or benches. Even as late as 1624, an inventory of Gilling Castle in Yorkshire listed thirty-five stools but only two chairs. But long before this date joiners had developed the medieval chest into a chair with a box in the seat. The most famous—and earliest known—example is the Coronation Chair in Westminster Abbey, first used by Edward I in the thirteenth century. While the Coronation Chair is oak—as are most chairs fashioned by medieval joiners—the "thrown" chairs (elaborately ornamented with knobs and rings) of the turners of the period were made of ash, elm, and yew because turners found oak too tough for their lathes, as well as brittle when cut across the grain.

Both turners and joiners benefited by a change in fashion at the end of Elizabeth I's reign—the substitution of stools for the wall benches that had lined one side of medieval dining tables. While stools enabled a diner to sit down or get up without disturbing his companions, they were uncomfortable. As a result, backs were added to stools, and these "backstools" eventually became known as side chairs. Originally, they were placed in front of tables consisting of boards resting on trestles which were removed after meals. Then, in the sixteenth century, tables supported by legs became permanent fixtures in the center of a room and table tops became either oval or round.

Tables were not the only household furnishings to undergo changes in appearance in the sixteenth century. This was due to the influence of Continental craftsmen who migrated to England at the invitation of the Tudors and Church officials. These artisans, imbued with the spirit of the Renaissance, filled abbeys, cathedrals, and the mansions that were replacing feudal castles with magnificently carved woodwork and intricately decorated furniture.

Native craftsmen soon learned all the newcomers had to teach. Their lesson proved profitable during the reign of Elizabeth I when the exploits of Drake and other gentlemen-adventurers filled the royal coffers with treasure taken from Spanish galleons and foreign trade led to the rise of a

*Tudor oak stool.*

BELOW: *An oak table, made about 1690.*

*An oak and walnut cradle, first half of the 17th century.*

wealthy merchant class. There was a demand for luxurious domestic furnishings and woodworkers filled it with richly carved chairs, ornately decorated cabinets, huge beds, and other elaborate pieces. While all this furniture owed much to foreign influence, it had "a national sturdiness of character inseparable from English art at all periods."

Much of the new-styled furniture was constructed of oak. However, little of it was made of home-grown timber which, while excellent for ship and house building, was too coarse for paneling or fine furniture. Therefore, as early as the fourteenth century, English craftsmen imported oak (wainscot) from Northern Europe, and by Elizabethan times were using it exclusively when catering to wealthy patrons. Meanwhile, joiners continued to use native ash, beech, and elm for their inexpensive wares which were now competing with furniture held together with hand-hammered nails.

Late in the sixteenth century upholstered furniture became fashionable. But the idea of using textiles on household furnishings was not new. Loose cushions had been strewn on medieval benches to make them more comfortable, and these probably served their purpose as well as the Elizabethan ones of velvet and satin edged with silver and gold lace and ornamented with pearls. "The fashion of cushioned chayrs is taken up in every merchant's house," wrote Sir John Harrington in 1597 and, by the early seventeenth

8

century, luxurious upholstered furniture was commonplace in the homes of the wealthy.

Actually, the combination of textiles and wood was employed in England long before the Stuart period. An inventory of 1466 describes "a chaire of tymbre astate (a high-backed wooden chair with arms) covered w$^t$ blu clothe of gold" and one finished in "purpell satyn." The chances are that these materials were secondhand, for Edward VI's footstool was covered with His Majesty's old gown, while in 1614 the Earl of Nottingham ordered his servants to cut to pieces his "embrodied cloke" and use it "to embroder some furniture for the howse withall."

At first, fabric-covered seat furniture was the province of the coffer maker but eventually became the work of a specialized craftsman—the upholder or upholsterer. Granted a charter by Edward IV in 1465, the upholsterers originally dealt in secondhand goods and evidently continued to do so for many years before covering furniture or providing the trade with materials for stuffing. Even as late as 1598, Bitchin Lane, London, "in the reigne of Henry the sixt, had yee for the most part dwelling Fripperers or Upholders that solde olde apparell and householde stuffe." Over the years the upholsterers became honored craftsmen—one of their number, Sir Bartholomew James, serving as Lord Mayor of London.

However, although upholstering became an important part of furniture-making, many members of the craft continued to deal in secondhand goods. For example, the trade card of Samuel Phene, "Upholder and Sworn Appraiser of the Golden Plow, the corner of Little Moorgate, London wall," informed the public that he "buys and sells, new and old reasonable . . . all sorts of goods . . . and undertakes funerals private or public."

Actually, Phene's willingness to undertake funerals merely indicated that he could furnish the black cloths custom dictated should be hung on the

*A walnut stool, about 1690. Upholstered furniture became popular at this time.*

walls of a house of mourning. These cloths were not sold but rented and provided upholsterers with a source of income.

William Cauty, "at the sign of the Chair and Curtain, the West End of Somerset House in the Strand," also solicited funerals, although, if his advertisements are to be believed, he should have been so busy that he could not leave his establishment:

> Bedsteads of every kind, sofas and chairs, finished as no Vermin of any Denomination can possible exist in either (Warranted Gratis) by a new and infaillable method, never before found out, and done nowhere else but at the above shop . . . Funerals performed to any Place in Great Britain.

But neither Cauty's "new and infaillable method" nor his readiness to serve patrons outside London brought him success. In fact, he was unable to pay his taxes in 1789, the collector noting beside his name, "poor, give him time."

During the Commonwealth, when a Puritan "had no starch in his linen, no gay furniture in his house," there was little demand for either carved or upholstered furniture. Nevertheless, turners and joiners who specialized in simple household furnishings found a ready market for their wares. Certain products such as the leather-covered chairs garnished with nails made by the turners of Buckinghamshire and other pieces fashioned by provincial craftsmen who had not been influenced by Continental designs actually won official approval.

While country craftsmen used local woods, London's fashionable furniture makers began working in walnut after the Restoration. Their creative talents, freed from the repression of Puritan austerity, developed new forms to serve old functions, and, influenced by the techniques of the Huguenot craftsmen who had followed Charles II to England, the London artisans met the demand for luxurious household furnishings. From their shops came writing desks for ladies, candlestands, and other specialized items, along with state beds and more comfortable and graceful chairs.

Among the latter were cane chairs. While all other chairs were fashioned by craftsmen who worked with joiners, cane-chair makers operated their own shops. They used imported French walnut for the frames of their expensive chairs and beech, either painted, japanned, or stained to simulate walnut, for their cheaper wares. Cane chairs sold well and, over the years, their structural features underwent many changes, as did their ornamentation.

Although cane furniture became less popular after 1700, it found a ready market in the provinces and the American colonies, despite the competition

*James II royal armchair with caned seat and back.*

of the wicker chairs made by basket weavers. Because the craftsmen who worked with cane felt that the basket weavers were infringing upon their privileges, they petitioned the joiners' guild—with which they were affiliated —to take action against them. But the basket weavers ignored the charges and continued to make wicker chairs as they had done since medieval times.

Meanwhile, London joiners and carvers were creating elegant furniture. Much of their work after 1685 shows the influence of the French wood-workers who had migrated to England following the revocation of the Edict of Nantes. Many of these artisans had designed furniture for the magnificent palaces of Louis XIV and all had been trained to produce richly ornamented pieces to harmonize with the sumptuous interiors favored by *Le Grand Monarque*. Besides inspiring native craftsmen to design ornately decorated wares, the exiles brought about an increase in the use of upholstery, the materials coming from the looms of Huguenot refugees who had established a silk-weaving industry in the Spitalfields section of London.

LEFT: *An example of marquetry, a commode by Pierre Langlois.* RIGHT: *This Adam cabinet veneered in satinwood, yew, and other woods was made about 1780.*

Although the immigrant craftsmen were masters of the art of using exotic woods to decorate furniture, English artisans successfully imitated their skill in veneering, parquetry, and marquetry. In all these processes, wood of a pleasing texture, color, or grain is fixed upon a carcass of another wood: veneering consists of gluing large thin slabs of fine wood over an inferior base; in parquetry small pieces of veneer are inlaid on the surface of a valuable wood; marquetry—the richest of all veneering methods—is the art of arranging inlays of colored wood in geometric or floral designs. The "blossoms" of the latter are frequently fashioned from inlaid mother-of-pearl or ivory.

The demand for lighter and more delicate furniture ornamented with veneer marked the end of the joiner's dominance of English furniture-making and the rise of a new craftsman—the cabinetmaker. However, joiners continued to make bedsteads and wainscot furniture embellished with fret and molding. Occasionally, their wares were decorated with carving, but carvers were finding it more profitable to work with cabinetmakers who provided patrons with richly carved furniture as well as veneered, painted, and japanned pieces.

Actually, skilled carvers had more work than they could handle in the latter part of the seventeenth century. The destruction caused by the Great

London Fire of 1666 created a tremendous demand for their talents. As a result, such master craftsmen as Grinling Gibbons (who worked with Sir Christopher Wren in the rebuilding of both secular and religious buildings) were far too busy to ally themselves with furniture makers. Incidentally, Gibbons, who specialized in swags of flowers and fruit, foliage, and birds, working with equal skill in lime, oak, pear, or boxwood, did some of his finest work for Wren. Moreover, he personally trained those who assisted him and thus had a lasting influence on the development of English wood-carving.

Certain late-seventeenth-century carvers were not interested in working for either cabinetmakers or architects. These individuals confined themselves to carving frames for mirrors, now an important element in interior decoration. Still others had formed an alliance with gilders, for ornately gilt furniture had become fashionable. This was a most practical partnership— what one craftsman carved, the other gilded. However, a few carvers did

*Staircase in pine, ash, and oak by Grinling Gibbons, about 1677.*

*William and Mary finely figured and faded walnut bureau bookcase.*

*English cabinetmakers, influenced by Continental craftsmen, employed exotic woods to make case furniture in the early 18th century. This mulberry cabinet is typical of the change that began during the reign of William and Mary.*

LEFT: *Early 18th-century walnut tallboy.* RIGHT: *Queen Anne walnut bachelor's chest, a lowboy. Workmen of this period simplified foreign imports to create a style that blended elegance and comfort.*

their own gilding. In 1699, John Pelletier, "Carver & Guilder," submitted a bill ". . . For Carving and guilding 4 frames for four Marble Tables" commissioned for the palace at Kensington.

Just as English craftsmen absorbed the techniques of Huguenot woodworkers, they borrowed and adapted from the Dutch artisans who accompanied William of Orange to England when Parliament offered him the Crown. Under the influence of such men as Daniel Marot, a French woodworker who had plied his trade in the Netherlands, native artisans combined the over-ornate decorations of the Louis XIV style with Chinese forms introduced by Dutch merchants. For example, the legs that supported the cabinets ordered by wealthy patrons to display their collections of Oriental porcelain ended in claw-and-ball feet. This motif was derived from the traditional Chinese representation of a three-toed dragon's claw holding a jewel. Similarly, English craftsmen adopted the cabriole leg which also originated in the Orient. They used this leg—whose curve arches suddenly outward before tapering gracefully to the foot—most successfully to support chairs and tables.

Working in walnut, London cabinetmakers produced a wide variety of furniture during the William and Mary period. From their shops came highback, banister-back, and Dutch-back chairs; butterfly, gate-leg, and tavern tables; settees and slant-top desks; and various types of beds. In addition to these pieces—the most comfortable furniture made up to that time—they fashioned two new types of case furniture. These were the highboy and the lowboy—actually chests set off the floor by legs.

Although Dutch influence dominated English furniture-making during the reign of "Good Queen Anne" (1702-1714), native craftsmen modified and simplified foreign importations. In the process they created a style that blended both elegance and comfort. Formal lines gave way to curves and, if straight lines were employed, they were softened by rounded corners. With the exception of massive tapestried beds ornamented with plumes or classical designs in the four corners, furniture became lighter, slightly higher, and more rectangular.

While the case furniture made during the "Age of Walnut" was beautifully designed and craftsmen showed great skill in fashioning cyma curves, scalloped aprons, broken pediment tops enclosing a flaming urn, and fan-shaped shell carvings, the chair is the most representative piece of the Queen Anne period. Both the luxurious wing chair (originally designed to cut drafts) and the utilitarian Windsor chair were introduced. The former was made by fashionable cabinetmakers who employed upholsterers to cover the frame with either leather or fabrics, while the latter was the work of both city turners and their fellow craftsmen in the provinces. Besides creating new chairs, woodworkers now began to construct traditional types in a more comfortable fashion, spooning their backs to fit the body, flaring the arms, and making the seats narrower at the rear than in the front.

The eighteenth century has been called the "Golden Age of Furniture" with good reason. The prosperity resulting from England's military triumphs during Anne's reign not only made it possible for the aristocracy to build large town and country residences but also enabled the middle class to raise its standard of living. As a result, there was a tremendous demand for household furnishings throughout the Georgian Period—a demand that was satisfied by the most outstanding craftsmen in the history of English furniture-making.

In their shops near St. Paul's Churchyard, in Soho, and other centers of their craft, these master artisans fashioned traditional pieces for conservative customers and catered to patrons who wanted the latest style. While certain individuals continued to specialize in chair and cabinetmaking, or upholstering, others operated establishments where all these crafts were practiced.

However, the owners of large shops rarely worked at the bench but employed joiners, turners, carvers, "and a vast army of the other mechanic branches" who made the furniture for which they have become famous. Even Chippendale, Hepplewhite, and Sheraton, who have given their names to three of the most popular furniture styles, have unwarranted reputations as master craftsmen.

Traditionally, this trio is credited with fashioning the finest furniture made in England between 1750 and 1800. But legend is stronger than fact. Chippendale created only a few pieces of furniture and even fewer of the

LEFT: *The early 18th-century wing chair was designed to cut drafts.* RIGHT: *Georgian chair with cabriole legs in walnut, upholstered in Fulham tapestry.*

furniture designs attributed to him; experts have failed to discover a single article that can be definitely assigned to Hepplewhite; while Sheraton never had a shop of his own.

As a matter of fact, much of the Georgian furniture cherished by collectors and displayed in museums is the work of unknown artisans who toiled twelve to fourteen hours a day for low wages in the shops of fashionable cabinetmakers. However, bills, city directories, labels, ledgers, letters, newspaper advertisements, and trade cards have enabled antiquarians to identify a number of the hundreds of furniture makers who worked in England during the eighteenth century.

One of the richest sources of information about these artisans is the Royal Household accounts where the bills of the master craftsmen commissioned by the Crown are recorded. While the names of certain individuals appear only a few times in the accounts, the names of others are mentioned frequently. Among those in the latter group is Gerritt Jensen, who served as cabinetmaker to the Royal Household during four reigns—from that of Charles II to the end of Queen Anne's. Jensen, who decorated his furniture with marquetry, inlaid metal, and japanning, also provided royalty with mirrors, his commission describing him as "Cabinett-maker and glass-seller."

Thomas Roberts, a joiner, also served the Crown for many years. He fashioned a "large rich fire skreene" for Windsor Castle; stools for Hampton Court; a "rich chair of state, the top of the back carved with a lion and unicorn and shields, cypher and crown, and sceptres, the lower part carved rich and all gilt" for Queen Anne's coronation; and "eighteen chairs of the best walnut tree . . . fully carved and polished" for George I's dining room in 1717.

While Roberts' foliated scrolls on seat rails show great control of ornamentation, his work does not compare with that produced at the *Golden Spread Eagle* by Benjamin Goodison, who numbered both royalty and aristocrats among his patrons. An outstanding craftsman, Goodison is famous for richly carved tables—some with marble tops—mirror frames, and the use of metal accessories on his case pieces. Upon Goodison's death his son Benjamin, Junior, continued the business with his father's nephew and former partner, Benjamin Parran. But their association was short-lived and Parran took over the firm.

The partnership of John Gumley and James Moore was more successful. Although they differed in personality—Gumley sought publicity but the only known newspaper reference to Moore is the report of his death in the *British Gazetteer* for October 22, 1726—they worked well together. Gumley became famous for his mirrors, Moore for his gilt gesso furniture.

Before entering into partnership with Moore, Gumley constantly advertised "all sorts of cabinet work" but specialized in supplying mirrors to the nobility. Among his customers was the first Duke of Devonshire, who paid £200 for a pair of mirrors in 1703. When the duke paid his bill, Gumley realized that his profit would have been greater if he had not had to purchase the glass. Therefore he decided to open his own glasshouse. Lacking the necessary capital, he persuaded a group of London merchants to join in the venture and built a factory in Lambeth.

By 1712 Gumley was so well known for his mirrors that Richard Steele suggested in *The Spectator* that those seeking mirrors should deal "with my diligent Friend & Neighbour Mr. Gumley." Evidently, a great many people took Steele's advice because in 1714—the same year that he became associated with Moore—Gumley established a showroom in the upper part of the New Exchange in the Strand.

Steele's article "Mr. Gumley's Glass Gallery over the New Exchange" which appeared in *The Lover*, May 13, 1715, provides proof that Gumley not only sold mirrors "for a trifle" but also carried a full line of furniture. "In the midst of the walk," wrote Steele, "are set in order a long row of rich tables on many of which lie cabinets, inlaid or wholly made of corals, ambers, in like Parts."

Gumley was delighted with this publicity, which probably led to the

LEFT: *Chippendale giltwood mirror.*
RIGHT: *Early 18th-century lacquer cabinet on giltwood stand.*

partners being appointed royal tradesmen after Jensen's retirement. Because certain of the mirrors "ffestoon finely done with carved and gilt work" the partners produced have "Gumley" carved on their frames or scratched upon the lower part of the glass, it is evident that Gumley took the credit for their manufacture.

Thanks to royal patronage, wealthy clients, and his glasshouse, Gumley accumulated a fortune. As a result, he was able to give his daughter Anna Maria a large dowry when she married the Earl of Bath. Anna was a source of publicity for her father—but it was unfavorable. "Lacking any good and agreeable quality but beauty," Anna's disagreeable disposition inspired Alexander Pope's poem "The Looking Glass." Pope suggested that since Gumley was a looking-glass maker, he should fashion one for Anna so that she could see herself as others did:

> "Could the sire, renowned in
>     glass, produce
> One faithful mirror for his
>     daughter's use."

*William Kent "dolphin" gilt-wood side table with oriental lacquer top, about 1730.*

RIGHT: *The Thomas Chippendale Harewood Desk—one of the most magnificent pieces produced in his shop.*

Meanwhile, Moore was making gesso furniture. Gesso is a composition of whiting, linseed oil, and glue which is applied thickly as a decorative coating on wood and is easily carved, gilded, or painted when it hardens. Moore was an excellent carver and his gilt gesso tables were avidly sought by both royalty and the wealthy. Paying little attention to contemporary fashion, Moore created original designs, then varied them.

Typical of his work is the gilt table made for Buckingham Palace. Its gesso-covered top is decorated with leaf-shaped ornaments and carries the crown cypher of George I (as does the apron) and both members are carved with representations of the rose and thistle. Moore's name is incised above the crown as it is in several surviving examples of his furniture. Why he failed to place his name on all his work is unknown, but by comparing the signed pieces with others of like workmanship, authorities have definitely assigned them to Gumley's retiring but talented partner.

Because of Gumley and Moore's reputation they were chosen by architect William Kent to construct some of the furniture he designed for Kensington Palace. The firm's accounts reveal that between 1723 and 1725, the partners supplied Kent with "four large sphinx stands for tables" and other articles. Gumley and Moore probably would have continued to furnish English palaces and homes with masterpieces for years if Moore had not died of "a Wound on his Head, which he received by a Fall as he was walking in the Street" in 1726.

Moore's will left his "materialls of Trade" to his son James. The younger Moore must have used them well for in 1732 he was appointed chair and cabinetmaker to Frederick, Prince of Wales. Meanwhile, Gumley took

William Turing as a partner, although he seems to have had a business arrangement with his mother, Mrs. Elizabeth Gumley. The firm of Gumley and Turing was dissolved when the senior partner died a year after it was formed, and Mrs. Gumley became associated with Turing.

Like her son, Mrs. Gumley received an appointment as cabinetmaker to the Crown. However, neither the furniture made by Gumley and Turing for George II nor the bills they submitted met with official approval and the commission as royal tradesmen was revoked.

While Thomas Chippendale's influence on furniture-making is well documented, little is known about him as an individual. In fact, there is no known record "from which it would be possible to imagine his appearance, or manners, or personal character." Born in either 1717 or 1718 in Otley, Yorkshire, where his family had been woodworkers for generations, Chippendale was probably taught his craft by his father, John Chippendale, a joiner. Then, when he was about twenty years old, Thomas went to London.

Nothing is known of his activities until 1748, the year in which his marriage to his first wife, Catherine Redshaw, was recorded in the register of St. George's Chapel, Mayfair. Other parish accounts reveal that in the following year Chippendale rented a house in Conduit Court where he opened a shop. In 1754 he moved to St. Martin's Lane, a fashionable throughfare where Sir Joshua Reynolds, the painter, and Louis Francois Roubiliac, the sculptor, had studios. Among Chippendale's other neighbors was Edward France, listed as an "upholder" in the directories of the day.

21

SAINT PETER'S COLLEGE LIBRARY
JERSEY CITY. NEW JERSEY 07306

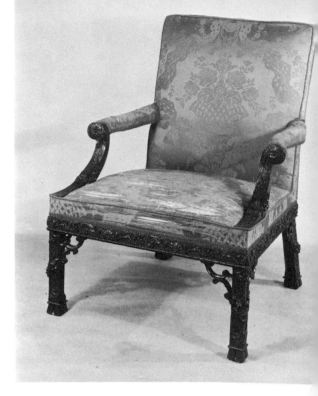

*One of a set of four mahogany library chairs attributed to Thomas Chippendale.*

Strangely enough, while France's name and address—and those of other minor craftsmen—appear in these publications, Chippendale is not mentioned, despite the fact that by 1755 he was renting three houses in St. Martin's Lane where he conducted his business until his death in 1799. But although no directory listed his thriving establishment, its location became known throughout England in 1754. In that year Chippendale issued the first edition of the *Gentleman and Cabinet-Maker's Director*.

The *Director* was the first book of furniture design to be published by an English cabinetmaker. However, William Kent, Batty Langley, William Jones, and other master builders had included drawings of furniture in their architectural texts. These men were primarily concerned with furniture that would harmonize with the spacious interiors they designed. Chippendale, on the other hand, conceived the *Director* as a catalog of the pieces he carried in stock, of designs he could make to order, and as a guidebook for his fellow craftsmen.

In planning his "large collection of the most Elegant and Useful designs of Household Furniture," Chippendale—who was always conscious of changing taste—turned to new fashions: the Gothic, revived by Horace Walpole; the Chinese, inspired by English trade and travel in the Orient; and the rococo, developed in France during Louis XV's reign. The rococo with its multiplicity of decorative motifs—the acanthus leaf, shells, scrolls, and other ornamentation—greatly appealed to Chippendale. However, few of the rococo designs in the *Director* were drawn by him, most being the work of Matthais Lock.

No man was better qualified for the task. Lock was not only a master carver but also he had pioneered in the creation of rococo furniture long before Chippendale adopted "the new French style." Because Lock published several books "useful to the carver" before the mid-1750's and after the late 1760's, it is thought he worked exclusively for Chippendale in the period between these dates. Lock's books, along with those examples of his drawings that have survived, stamp him as the most outstanding draftsman among eighteenth-century furniture designers. However, despite his skill, Lock has never received the acclaim he deserves.

The plates in the *Director* depicted a wide variety of furniture and are the source of Chippendale's reputation for creating the style that bears his name—beautifully proportioned pieces whose graceful outlines belie their strength and solidity. Moreover, Chippendale furniture is "tempered by French subtleties . . . having here and there, as in the fret-work of the chair-legs and angles, a suggestion of the East."

Curiously, although Chippendale is traditionally associated with mahogany, this wood is not mentioned in the descriptive notes that precede the plates. In fact, there is only one mention of wood in the notes which are filled with detailed instructions for copying the designs, for lacquering in the Chinese manner, and for gilding picture frames. Chippendale probably

*Chippendale furniture covers a wide range of styles.*

wrote this material himself, for, while it is practical, it contains many spelling and grammatical errors. On the other hand, the lengthy preface must have been the work of one of Chippendale's patrons, for it is sprinkled with classical allusions and written in a pedantic style.

English cabinetmakers ignored the preface and, following the notes, copied the designs shown in the plates. As a result, very little of the well-made furniture in the Chippendale style can be definitely attributed to the compiler of the *Director*. Actually, it is doubtful if Chippendale worked with tools following publication of his book. He was far too busy waiting on customers who were willing to pay $1,500 for a lavishly carved mirror frame, supervising his designers, and overseeing workmen to spend any time at the bench. Fortunately, James Rannie—whom he must have taken into partnership shortly after opening his shop—relieved him of business details. Nevertheless, all did not go smoothly. Chippendale had difficulties with the Society of Upholsterers and, in April, 1775, the *Gentleman's Magazine* reported:

> *Saturday 5*
> A fire broke out in the workshop of Mr. Chippendale, a cabinet-maker near St. Martin's Lane, which consumed the same, wherein were the chests of 22 workmen.

Despite this fire—evidently in a detached building—business continued as usual and Chippendale issued a second edition of the *Director*. While this reprinting duplicated the original volume, the third edition published in 1762 contained many changes. Among these were the elimination of certain technical material and a new title page that made no reference to the

*This mahogany writing table on carved cabriole legs was pictured in the third edition of the* Director, *1762.*

*An Adam satinwood and marque-
try secretary.*

Chinese and Gothic styles which were going out of fashion. Previous title pages had described Chippendale as a cabinetmaker, but the new one identifies him as a "cabinet-maker and upholsterer" which shows that he was now furnishing fabrics for drapes, bed coverings, and chair covers.

Certain of the original plates do not appear in the third edition, others were redrawn, and while the rococo dominates, a number of new plates reflect Chippendale's acceptance of classical design—straight, square-section, tapering and fluted legs, block and lion feet, and such ornamental details as strings of husks.

After 1776 Chippendale worked closely with architect Robert Adam, who, inspired by the excavations at Pompeii, sparked the neo-classical movement in England. Although Adam was a snob and treated artisans he commissioned with contempt, he evidently had the highest regard for Chippendale as a craftsman, if not as an individual. Therefore, Chippendale was Adam's only associate who dealt directly with the architect's clients. While they might grumble over the amount of their bills—Chippendale's charges were apt to be higher than his estimates—or complain that delivery had not been made, none could find fault with his purchases. Masterpieces of design and workmanship, they also bore those distinctive features of legs, scroll ornament, and inlay typical of Chippendale's last period.

Meanwhile Rannie had died. Chippendale announced via the *Public Advertiser* that he intended to carry on the business but would offer at public auction on March 27, 1766, "a great variety of fine Cabinet Work . . . a Parcel of fine season'd Feathers; as well as the large unwrought stock. . . ."

25

*Adam serving table painted green and white with mahogany top.*

BELOW: *Mahogany cupboard by William Vile, about 1760.*

BELOW LEFT: *George III painted chair.* BELOW RIGHT: *George III giltwood chair.*

It appears that this auction was necessary to settle Rannie's estate, and Chippendale probably had no desire to enter into another partnership by the time the lawyers were satisfied. However, he found it impossible to conduct his business singlehanded and, in 1771, formed an alliance with Thomas Haig, a former clerk of Rannie's. Haig assumed the task of making out the bills and carefully described every item whether it was "A very large rich commode . . . the whole Elegantly Executed" or "6 Brass Cloak-pins."

Despite Haig's help, Chippendale found no time to rest. Moreover, besides being weary, he was having financial problems because customers were not paying their bills. Finally, worn out physically and mentally, Chippendale contracted tuberculosis and died in 1799.

While Chippendale's shop has long been considered the source of the finest English furniture in the rococo style, nothing produced there is equal to the pieces fashioned by two of his neighbors in St. Martin's Lane—William Vile and his partner, John Cobb. However, it is only in recent years that "the unchallenged supremacy of the Vile workshop in English cabinet-making of the mid-eighteenth century has been established."

Vile and Cobb formed their partnership in 1750 and it lasted until the former's retirement in 1765. A master carver, Vile is famous for enriching his pieces with fretted detail, pendants, wreaths, swags and festoons of flowers and fruit, and masks. Cobb's specialty was furniture in the classical style embellished with marquetry.

While Vile and Cobb's furniture made for London mansions and country estates is outstanding in both craftmanship and design, some of their best work was done for George III, who had been a customer of Vile's before assuming the Crown. One of their commissions was the remodeling of "His Majesty's Great Medal Case" into two separate cabinets by removing the open shelf section in its center. Experts have determined that Vile used the two original carved ends of the case to enclose one cabinet and made two new sides for the other.

The cabinet with the original sides is now displayed in New York City's Metropolitan Museum of Art, that with the new in the Victoria and Albert Museum in London. John Bradburn probably carved the latter—an attribution made on the basis of a clock case fashioned by Bradburn for George III in 1765. Bradburn was one of the firm's most valued employees and Vile thought so much of him that he left Bradburn a legacy in his original will. However, when Vile retired and Bradburn was chosen to replace him as cabinetmaker to the Crown, Vile was so incensed because one of his workmen was considered his equal that he withdrew the bequest.

Cobb's reaction to Bradburn's appointment is unknown but it probably

*Georgian tripod fret-carved octagonal tilt-top table stands on snake feet and has a birdcage support.*

RIGHT: *Named for the notorious Margaret Rudd, mechanical dressing tables like this are described in Hepplewhite's Guide.*

infuriated him. He had little respect for the ability of others, being "a singularly haughty character" and "one of the proudest men in England." Nevertheless, he was a clever craftsman whose marquetried bombé commodes, neo-classical chairs, and other pieces—many of which are ornamented by an inverted honeysuckle device which serves as a "signature"—compare favorably with the vigorously carved and well-designed mahogany rococo furniture of his partner.

Because of the frequent mention of Cobb in E. T. Smith's *Nollekins and his Times*, much is known about Cobb's personality. Smith reports that Cobb dressed in the latest fashion even when "strutting through his workshop giving orders to his men." While many people considered Cobb boastful, George III, who frequently employed him for cabinet work "of the most elaborate and expensive sort," merely smiled "at his pomposity." However, Cobb did incur royal displeasure while making alterations to His Majesty's library. Finding the book he wanted blocked by a ladder, the king asked Cobb to get it for him.

Typically, Cobb turned to an assistant and thundered, "Fellow, hand me that book!"

"Just a minute," interposed the king. "What is this man's name?"

"Jenkins, Sire," replied the astonished Cobb.

"Then," said George, "Jenkins, *you* shall hand me the book."

As indicated, Cobb specialized in marquetry but he was also an expert carver. Frequently, he shared the task of carving with Sederin Aiken, one of his employees who won the praise of Robert Adam for his work on doors, windows, and architraves. While Cobb himself probably did no

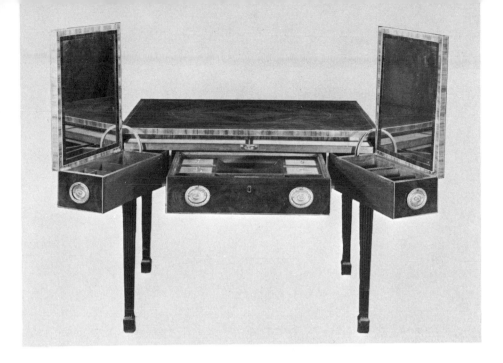

upholstering, he furnished Horace Walpole with tapestry chairs and a carpet in 1770. By this date his shop was one of London's finest and, as a result, when Cobb died in 1778 he had been so successful that he left his wife the interest on twenty thousand pounds, stipulating "that the principal twenty thousand pounds stock is never to be broke into . . . my intent being that there should always be the interest aforesaid to support the name of Cobb as a private gentleman."

Of all the men who influenced furniture design in England, the least is known about George Hepplewhite. Not even the date of his birth has been established. In fact, the only definite information we have about Hepplewhite is that he served an apprenticeship with Gillow of Lancaster; that his place of business was Redcross Street, London; and that his wife Alice continued to operate his firm after her husband's death in 1786 under the name of A. Hepplewhite and Company.

Hepplewhite could not have served his apprenticeship in a finer shop than that of the Gillows. Robert Gillow, a joiner who had founded the firm, and his son Robert, inventor of the telescopic dining-room table, supplied excellent furniture not only to local patrons and their London showroom but also to foreign countries. However, despite his training, Hepplewhite probably never would have achieved fame if his wife had not published his book of furniture designs—*The Cabinet-maker and Upholsterer's Guide.*

The first edition of the *Guide* appeared in 1788—two years after Hepplewhite's death—and was the largest volume of its type to appear in twenty

*Hepplewhite offered the first sideboard consisting of a single unit. This one is inlaid mahogany. The platter is Mason's Ironstone.*

years. Although many of its three hundred illustrations show that Hepplewhite had been influenced by Chippendale, the avowed purpose of the *Guide* was to show cabinetmakers "how to apply Adam's principles of elegance combined with utility." But despite its borrowings from Chippendale and its summary of Adam's neo-classicism, the *Guide* contained much original material. As a result, Hepplewhite popularized the easy chair, set the fashion for painted and lacquered furniture, and offered the first sideboard consisting of a single unit in place of an assembly of a side table flanked by two pedestals.

However, Hepplewhite showed his greatest ingenuity in the designing of chairs which he supported on plain, reeded square legs that tapered to a spade foot. While these light, delicate, and graceful chairs give the impression that they are fragile, they are very sturdy.

Whether or not Hepplewhite was the first to design the shield-back chair is a moot question, but no one used this formula—or oval and heart-back—to better advantage. Usually, these backs were plain, only the shield being ornamented. Provincial craftsmen who avidly studied the *Guide*—which was reissued with a few modifications in 1789—were content to leave the middle splats plain or pierced, but in London shops they were carved with wheat ears, classical urns, drapery, or "Prince of Wales" feathers. This last motif, although a characteristic of the Hepplewhite style, did not originate with the author of the *Guide*, having been used as the cresting of looking glasses during the reign of George I.

Hepplewhite favored mahogany chairs (which he noted would be covered with "horse hair, plain, striped, chequered, etc., at pleasure") but suggested beech for painted chairs. Actually, he preferred painted to carved furniture, although the Guide often combines both carving and painting on a single piece. This is particularly true of Hepplewhite-style beds whose cornices, whether simply or ornately ornamented, "may be either of mahogany carved, carved and gilt, or painted and japanned." But even if the cornices were painted, the turned, tapered, reeded or fluted bedposts were of mahogany "with the enrichments carved."

From the beginning, the *Guide* sold well, both country craftsmen and city cabinetmakers finding it a source of fashionable designs and technical information. In 1794, a third edition was published containing many new drawings to counteract Sheraton's criticism of Hepplewhite's designs. There is no certainty that Hepplewhite drew the plates for the third edition of the *Guide* or that he is responsible for the drawings attributed to him in *The Cabinet-maker's London Book of Prices* issued in 1788. However, these designs played an important part in making his name synonymous with a furniture style—a style as popular today as it was in the late Georgian Period.

Not only has Thomas Sheraton been carelessly credited with fashioning a tremendous amount of furniture (it is almost certain he produced nothing after 1790) but also his name has been given to a style popular in the last decade of the eighteenth century, despite the fact that he did not originate it.

LEFT: *Sheraton satinwood bookcase.*

BELOW: *Hepplewhite serpentine commode.*

Sheraton was born at Stockton-on-Tess in 1751. Nothing is known of his early life and, although his published designs reveal him to be an outstanding draftsman, there is no evidence that he received formal training in drawing and geometry as a boy. However, one of the few personal references Sheraton makes in his numerous writings infers that he was apprenticed to a cabinetmaker: " . . . having possessed a strong attachment and inclination to carving in my youth, I was necessarily inclined to make attempts in this art, and, succeeding in some degree, I was employed in the county occasionally in it."

Although Sheraton describes himself as a "mechanic," he probably never worked with his hands after coming to London in 1790. Perhaps if he had, his life would have been easier. As it was, he lived in abject poverty, a failure in all things. Few pupils or customers visited his Wardour Street residence after reading his trade card that informed the public that Sheraton "teaches perspective, architecture and ornaments, makes designs for cabinetmakers, sells all kinds of drawing books." Nor did Sheraton's preaching as a Baptist create interest. Finally, the series of books dealing with furniture design to which he devoted the last sixteen years of his life—and on which his fame rests—were not commercially successful.

Sheraton's first book *The Cabinet-Maker and Upholsterer's Drawing Book* was published in parts between 1791 and 1794. The first two parts are devoted to geometric designs, the third section was intended "to exhibit the present taste of furniture, and at the same time, to give workmen some assistance in the manufacturing part of it."

In order to accomplish these aims Sheraton went from shop to shop sketching designs and collecting information. As a result, the volume illustrates a wide variety of furniture, ranging from perfectly proportioned simple pieces to over-ornamented wares that lack grace, and includes far more technical information than any similar work. Sheraton, who was acutely aware of current fashions, also included advice for those who wished to furnish their homes in the latest taste. He disposed of Chippendale's and Hepplewhite's design books by calling them "now wholly antiquated and laid aside" and bluntly stated that Robert Manwaring's *Chairmakers' Guide* contained nothing "but what an apprentice boy may be taught in seven hours instruction."

Among the original contributions to furniture-making in the *Drawing Book* are: domed hoods on the upper sections of small desks; writing tables of exotic woods (designed for use by women); and several novelties including a "Summer Bed in Two Compartments." The latter—the prototype of the modern twin bed—consisted of two beds joined at the feet by an arch with a passageway between "so that two people could sleep separately in hot weather."

Even a casual examination of the *Drawing Book* reveals that Sheraton excelled in the designing of chairs. His chairs, whether made of mahogany, painted or gilted beechwood, or cane, give an impression of grace and lightness that charms the eye. Their square backs were a Sheraton innova-

*Pair of Sheraton painted and gilded chairs.*

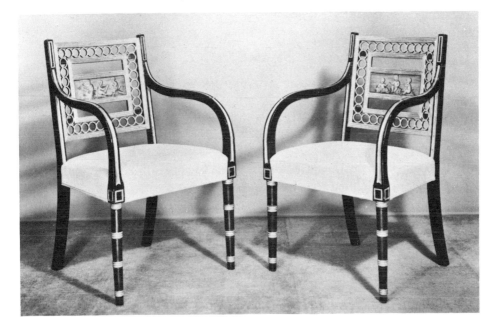

RIGHT: *An example of harlequin furniture—these library steps fold into a chair.*

BELOW: *Sheraton sofa table in mahogany, crossbanded in satinwood.*

tion and replaced the shield- and oval-back formula of Hepplewhite. Generally, Sheraton divided the square backs on his chairs into three sections, the central one being filled with ornamentation based on classical motifs.

In 1803, Sheraton published the *Cabinet Dictionary*, "an Explanation of all the Terms used in the Cabinet, Chair and Upholstery branches, containing a display of useful articles of furniture." It was an ambitious undertaking and Sheraton was hard pressed to find the funds to finance it. Unlike the *Drawing Book*, which showed Sheraton's ability to employ oval forms, contrast mahogany with lighter woods, and his sensitivity to foreign influences, the *Dictionary* is filled with bizarre designs.

The *Dictionary* shows Sheraton's fascination with "harlequin furniture" (pieces having a dual purpose): a library table that concealed a ladder; a combination dressing table, desk, and washstand; and an ottoman with "heating urns" below so "that the seat may be kept at a proper temperature in cold weather."

Actually, it is difficult to associate these extravagances with the Sheraton whose designs brought lightness and grace to English furniture. However, Clifford Musgrave, the eminent antiquarian, suggests that Sheraton's "fastidious inventive spirit, cramped by privation, found release in works of art of a richness, fantasy and beauty he was never to experience in the realities of his own life."

The debased taste of the *Dictionary* was merely a forerunner of the designs Sheraton illustrated in *The Cabinet-Maker, Upholsterer and General Artist's Encyclopedia* which he planned to issue in 125 parts. But only one part, covering A to C, appeared, being published in 1805, the year before Sheraton's death. Strangely enough, despite Sheraton's influence on cabinet-making, his death was practically ignored. However, a brief notice did appear in the *Gentleman's Magazine*:

> ...He was a honest well disposed man of an acute and enterprising disposition; but like many other self-taught authors, showing the want of regular education in his writings. He has left his family, it is feared in distressed circumstances.

*Sheraton game table and chessmen made of exotic woods.*

As indicated, Chippendale, Hepplewhite, and Sheraton—thanks to their design books—have overshadowed their contemporaries. Nevertheless, certain of the trio's competitors were not only makers of fine furniture but also authors of books that had a tremendous impact on furniture design. Among these craftsmen were William Ince and John Mayhew, who published the *Universal System of Household Furniture*, and Thomas Shearer, specialist in case pieces who did the plates for *Designs for Household Furniture*. Equally important are William Hallet, perhaps the most fashionable cabinet-maker during George III's reign; Giles Grendey, exporter of japanned furniture to the Continent; and George Seddon, master of the Joiners' Company who had "an understanding of the requirements of the needy and the luxurious, knowing how to satisfy them from the products of nature and the artistry of manufacture."

The term Regency has one meaning to historians and another to antiquarians. The former use it only to describe the years 1811 to 1820 when the future George IV ruled England as Prince Regent because of his father's insanity. On the other hand, the latter employ Regency as a descriptive term for all the decorative arts produced in England during the first three decades of the nineteenth century.

Because this was a period in which public taste changed frequently, the Regency style covers a wide variety of design. As originated by Henry Holland (1745-1808), the architect who furnished Carlton House for George IV when he was Prince of Wales, Regency furniture consisted of classical design tinctured with a dash of French craftsmanship. In time—whether made of mahogany or exotic woods—Regency furniture developed into solid pieces, simple in outline, featuring horizontal and vertical lines in their large uninterrupted surfaces, ornamentation of which was subdued. Gradually, this "Grecian severity" gave way to Gothic and Chinese revivals and the use of the Egyptian motifs shown in Thomas Hope's *Household Furniture*.

While Hope's book, and those of Peter and Michael Angelo Nicholson, Richard Brown, and George Smith were designed for use by craftsmen, Ackerman's *The Repository of the Arts*—published monthly between 1808 and 1828—was not only read by tradesmen but also by young ladies who made a hobby of painting and decorating small household furnishings. S. J. Fuller's shop, *The Temple of Fancy*, catered to these "artists," one of the first groups to engage in handicraft for pleasure. Fuller stocked among other items:

An extensive collection of handsome screens both Plain and Ornamented, Screen-poles, elegant Stands for Table-Tops and Chess-Boards,

LEFT: *Early Regency cylinder-top desk in faded mahogany with ormolu (brass made to imitate gold in appearance) gallery, about 1805.*

RIGHT: *Regency rosewood commode inlaid with brass and mounted with ormolu in the style of Le Gaigneur.*

Card-Racks . . . and White-Wood Boxes in a variety of shapes . . . with every requisite useful for Painting and Ornamenting the same.

Meanwhile, excellent furniture was being created by Elward, Marsh and Tatham, "Upholders of Mount Street," and Frederick Bogaert. The latter was a master carver "equally happy in his designs for furniture and other branches of interior decoration." Outstanding pieces were also produced in the large establishments of Morgan and Saunders, Tatem and Bailey, and Morel and Hughes, and in the shops of specialists. Among the latter was Louis le Gaigneur, maker of boule furniture, who owed his success to the patronage of Beau Brummell, prince of dandies.

While these artisans were fashioning furniture that prompted Sydney Smith to write, " . . . after banishing the heathen gods and their attributes pretty well from our poetry we are to introduce them . . . into our eating rooms, nurseries and staircases," country craftsmen were making furniture that owed little to archaeological fantasy.

As a matter of fact, rural woodworkers—with few exceptions—had always either ignored London fashions or adopted them belatedly. Moreover, makers of cottage furniture catered to conservative customers who desired sturdy pieces that would serve their purpose for years. Therefore, village craftsmen continued to produce utilitarian furniture from local woods during the Regency period as they had for centuries. For example, in High Wycombe, Buckinghamshire, generations of turners, benchmen, and framers had combined their skills to make Windsor chairs.

However, High Wycombe was not the only source of Windsors. Kitchen chairs of this type had been made throughout rural England since the 1500's. They originated when some unknown but ingenious country craftsman added a fourth leg to the traditional three-legged milking-stool and fixed a bent willow in the seat to support the back.

High Wycombe became famous for Windsors after 1805 when Samuel Treacher, a farmer, seeking to keep his hired hands busy during the winter, hired Thomas Widginton to teach them how to assemble chairs from parts made by professionals. From this humble beginning have come the sprawling furniture factories of present-day High Wycombe—Widginton established the first in 1810—that turn out thousands of Windsors annually by mass-production methods developed by Lucian Ercolini.

As the nineteenth century reached the halfway mark, the impact of the Industrial Revolution was being felt in both the large establishments of London cabinetmakers and the home shops of rural craftsmen. Actually, woodworking machines capable of carrying out practically all the processes now used in the large-scale manufacture of furniture had been patented by Sir Samuel Bentham between 1791 and 1793. In fact, as early as 1807, Thomas Hope had predicted a decline in English furniture-making "through the entire substitution of machinery to manual labour."

Hope was right. By 1820 only eleven master carvers were working in London and, by 1850, the handworker was replaced by the machine. However, the art of fashioning wood into well-designed, carefully-constructed household furnishings did not vanish from England. Today—as always—creative artisans are making hand-wrought furniture of great beauty in London shops.

These craftsmen use both traditional materials and the new products of technology in their search for new shapes and the perfection of old ones in order to provide more comfort to the body and greater pleasure to the eye. There is little doubt that this furniture would meet the approval of the carvers, cabinetmakers, chairmakers, gilders, joiners, and turners who preceded them, for it maintains the standards they set for their craft over the centuries.

# 2

## *Glass*

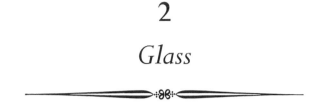

As Rome's mighty legions marched across Gaul, they were followed by glassmakers from Syria—where the art of blowing glass originated—seeking to expand their market. These artisans established glasshouses in the valleys of the Rhine and Seine Rivers and, by the end of the second century A.D., were exporting glass vessels to Britain.

Although this cross-Channel trade continued to flourish long after the decline of the Roman Empire, the "trunk beakers" and other wares of the Rhine-Seine glassfield had to compete with the products of the glassworks erected behind Hadrian's Wall during the Roman occupation of Britain. When the Roman troops were withdrawn to defend Italy against a threatened invasion by the Goths in A.D. 408, their glasshouses were taken over by native craftsmen who had learned the secrets of the craft from their conquerors. From their blowing tubes came various articles of bluish-green glass—the color varying in depth in proportion to the amount of impurities in the sand used in the manufacturing.

It is from *glas*, the Celtic word for the bluish-green color of these early wares, that the word glass is derived.

The floods of Teutonic invaders that engulfed Britain during the sixth and seventh centuries put out the glassmakers' fires, and the art of blowing glass was lost. However, it survived on the Continent and, as early as A.D. 678, the Bishop of Mayence (presently the city of Mainz, Germany), sent glassmakers to England to fashion windows for church property. While there are records of other glassmakers crossing the Channel, it was not until the thirteenth century that Norman craftsmen made a permanent settlement in the Weald, then a heavily wooded district extending across Kent, Surrey, and Essex. Not only did the beechwood stands of the Weald furnish fuel for their furnaces, but also the ashes of the bracken that covered its glens provided them with an excellent source of potash to fuse sand into glass.

Perhaps the first of the Wealden glassmakers was Laurence Vitrearius, who began making clear and colored glass in what is now Chiddingfold, Surrey, in A.D. 1226. An excellent craftsman, Vitrearius received an order about 1240 for both these kinds of glass for the new abbey at Westminster. Like all Norman glassmakers, Vitrearius made his panes by the "crown" process. This consisted of opening a bubble of glass at the end of the blowing rod which was rapidly rotated. This rotation caused the bubble—which was constantly reheated—to spread by centrifugal force into a more or less flat disc about four feet in diameter with a "bull's eye" in the middle. After cooling, diamond-shaped or rectangular panes were cut from the disc.

Vitrearius' son, William le Verrir, carried on his father's business until the end of the thirteenth century. Meanwhile, other Norman glassmaking families had established themselves in and around Chiddingfold. While the Chiddingfold craftsmen had competition from individuals such as John Glasewrythe who was making "brodeglass" in "Shuerwode" in 1380, the Normans controlled the manufacture of window glass in England until glassmakers from Lorraine who had been trained in the art of making stained glass settled in the Weald during the sixteenth century.

The Lorrainers' method of making window glass differed from that of the Normans. They employed the "broad" process—after shearing off the end of an elongated glass bubble, they cut it lengthwise, then flattened the cylinder. In addition to panes, the newcomers also produced "bottles, bowles, cuppis to drinck and such lyke" and by 1557 were working from patterns supplied by customers as well as furnishing stock glass vessels to peddlers who wandered over the countryside hawking their wares.

However, it was not until 1567, when John Carré of Antwerp secured a license from the English government to manufacture "glas such as is made in Fraunce," that the most skilful Lorrainers came to England. Carré, who hoped to corner the English glass market by making clear glass vessels in London and window glass in the Weald, imported members of the Hennezel, Thiétry, Thisac, and Houx families—all of whom proudly bore the title *gentilhommes verriers*.

Carré's Wealden operation was most successful. But the Norman glassmakers resented his Lorrainers, while the local iron founders complained that they were hard pressed to keep their furnaces glowing because the newcomers were using so much wood for fuel. However, both groups were powerless until Carré's death in 1572. Then, by threats of physical violence and plots to burn down glasshouses, they forced the Lorrainers to leave the Weald and ply their craft in other localities.

Meanwhile, Carré's London venture had run into difficulties. By 1570 it was obvious that his plan of using Lorrainers to fashion crystal wares of the type made on the Island of Murano near Venice—long the center of European glassmaking—was impractical. The reason was simple—Carré's craftsmen lacked the necessary skill. Therefore, to staff his glassworks at the Hall of the Crutched Friars, he imported six Venetians in 1571—the date that marks the permanent establishment of a crystal glass manufactory in England.

Among the glassmakers imported by Carré was Giacomo Verzelini, who was born in Venice in 1522. About 1549, having mastered his craft, he had migrated to Antwerp—then second only to Venice as a glassmaking center—where he became so successful that the well-to-do Vanburen family gave him permission to marry Elizabeth Vanburen in 1555. Because of Verzelini's social position and professional standing, Carré's proposition must have been very attractive to persuade the 50-year-old Venetian to leave Antwerp.

While evidence is lacking that Verzelini had an interest in the Crutched Friars glasshouse, he took control of it upon Carré's death, despite the fact that, as a foreigner, he had no right to own property. The wares he produced were of high quality, but London shopkeepers who were importing glass from the Continent to meet the ever-increasing demand gave him no encouragement. They reasoned that Verzelini's glass—which was less expensive than the foreign product—would reduce their profit. This may explain the mysterious fire that broke out on September 4, 1575, "about seven of the clocke," and destroyed the Crutched Friars glasshouse.

Verzelini outwitted his enemies by applying for a royal privilege. On December 15, 1575, Elizabeth I granted him a 21-year monopoly: "for the makynge of drynkynge glasses suche as be accustomablie made in the towne of Murano and hathe undertaken to teache and bringe vppe in the said Arte and knowledge of makynge the said drynkynge glasses oure naturall Sub-

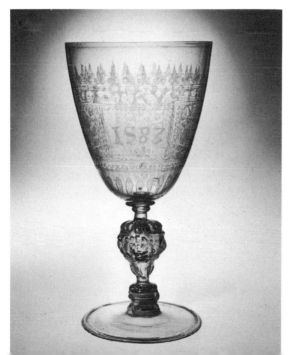

*Dated 1583, this is one of the nine known surviving engraved pieces fashioned by Verzelini.*

jectes." His privilege also forbade the importation of foreign glass.

Upon receiving this assurance of Royal support, Verzelini became an English citizen, rebuilt the Crutched Friars glasshouse, and opened a new works in Broad Street. His appointment as "Glassmaker to the Queen" increased the demand for his wares and, to meet it, he employed a staff of 150. However, it is doubtful if more than 20 of this number were master craftsmen.

Very few specimens of Verzelini's glass have survived. Those that have are elaborately engraved by the diamond-point technique and appear to be the work of a single individual—possibly Anthony de Lysle. The only engraver of glass known to have worked in England from 1580 to 1602, Lysle is thought not only to have worked for Verzelini but also to have engraved glasses for private customers. Lysle engraved pewter as well as glass and there is a record of his being censured by the Pewterers' Company for gilding pewter to give it the appearance of silver.

But the majority of Verzelini's assistants were honest men, proud of their association with "Mr. Jacob," as their master was known to all. Few left his service and parish registers show many a glassmaker's son was named for his father's employer. Mr. Jacob also had sons, but not one of the six was interested in glassmaking. While he was disappointed that there was no member of his family to carry on the business, Mr. Jacob continued to work until 1592, when he retired to his country estate in Kent. However, he spent the winter months in London in the house he had built near the Crutched Friars works. It was there that "the pattern of all glassmakers" died at the age of eighty-four on January 20, 1606.

Petitions requesting government action to stop "the making of glass by strangers and outlandish men" flooded Parliament in 1585. These appeals originated with shrewd promoters who wanted to secure control of English glassmaking. The first to achieve this goal was Sir Jerome Bowes, a former ambassador to Russia who took over Verzelini's operations following his retirement. When Sir Jerome's monopoly expired in 1606, his privileges were parceled out to both individuals and companies.

Anxious for profit, Sir Jerome's successors enlarged existing glassworks and built new ones. As a result, England's forests were consumed at an alarming rate and fear was expressed that, between the demands of iron smelters and glassmakers, soon there would not be enough timber to meet the Royal Navy's requirements.

As a matter of fact, Verzelini had experienced a shortage of beechwood to heat his pots, and, as early as 1586, coal had been used experimentally to make glass. But while the coal provided higher temperatures, its fumes discolored the molten metal. Then, in 1610, Sir William Slyngsby developed a coal-burning glass furnace that melted the metal in covered pots, thus pro-

LEFT: *Goblet attributed to Verzelini: probably engraved by Anthony de Lysle in 1577.* RIGHT: *Posset, milk curdled with ale or wine and spiced, was considered a cure-all in the 17th century. This posset glass with its applied stem and opposing double-loop handles combines the techniques of blowing and molding glass.*

tecting it from discoloration. The following year, Thomas Percivall—first to use coal successfully to fuse glass—and a group of associates were awarded a patent for an improved coal-burning furnace. They had perfected their invention by 1615 when a "Royal Proclamation Touching Glasses" prohibited the use of wood as a glassmaking fuel.

In 1618 Sir Robert Mansell, a retired admiral who had helped finance Percivall's experiments, was given authority to destroy all wood-burning glasshouses. However, when Mansell (after manipulations worthy of a modern tycoon) secured all existing glass monopolies in 1623 from James I, he ignored the law. Although his patent stipulated that he must use any "fewell whatsoever not being tymber or wood," he operated several glassworks fired by wood. On the other hand, Mansell insisted that his legal rights be upheld and frequently called upon the authorities to arrest those who dared to make glass or import it unless he had granted them a license.

Forced to defend his privilege from would-be rivals and inexperienced in the handling of creative craftsmen, Mansell underwent some trying years before he recouped the fortune he had spent in financing the development of the coal-burning furnace. An astute businessman, Mansell efficiently organized English glassmaking, but during his monopoly—which ended in 1655—little progress was made in glass manufacture. Moreover, Mansell's glassmen were content to copy Venetian and Continental forms, thus contributing nothing to the creation of a characteristic style of English glassware.

"Cristall" drinking vessels were in small demand between 1642 and 1649 while Roundhead battled Royalist during England's Civil War. However, by the time the Commonwealth was established, glass vessels were being produced in sufficient quantities to prompt Cromwell to tax glasshouses. The Lord Protector also abolished the charter the Worshipful Company of Glass-sellers had received from Charles I, by which that body controlled the sale of glass, and revoked Mansell's monopoly.

But within three months of Charles II's arrival in London a monopolist was benefiting from the Restoration. He was George Villars, second Duke of Buckingham (1628-1687), a master of political intrigue with an avid interest in science. Buckingham's first glassmaking venture was to finance a London manufactory where John de la Cam, a Master Doctor Ordinary to the King of France, produced a lime-soda glass that he advertised as "Christall de roache or Venice Christall." According to the agreement, the two were to share all profits equally for a "Terme of tenne yeares," but Cam withdrew from the partnership and went to Nijmegen, The Netherlands, where he established a glasshouse in 1688.

Meanwhile, Buckingham had secured patents giving him sole rights to the various processes of "makeing cristall" developed by Martin Clifford, Thomas Powlden, and Thomas Tilson. The Duke also acquired control of Tilson's method of making mirrors and began manufacturing mirror plate at his Vauxhall glasshouse which was under the management of John Bellingham, an Englishman who had learned his craft in the Low Countries.

While Tilson's process enabled Buckingham's gaffers to blow clearer drinking vessels than any previously made in England, they were tinged with color. Moreover, they lacked brilliancy and did not have the transparency of Continental glass. Therefore, the Worshipful Company of Glass-sellers—whose charter gave it control of glass manufacturers and retailers in and for seven miles around London—decreed that the glassworks under their jurisdiction should seek a formula for a "verrij Bright cleer and whit sound Mettall."

Not only did the Company order others to seek a process to improve English crystal but also it financed research by members of the recently formed Royal Society. Among the amateur glassmakers who conducted experiments for the Company were Dr. Christopher Merret, who in 1662

LEFT: *Although made in England about 1685, this lead glass goblet is decorated in the typical Venetian style of the period.* RIGHT: *One of a pair of engraved vessels produced by Ravenscroft within a year of the perfection of the lead glass formula.*

published *The Art of Glass* (a translation of Antonio Neri's *L'Arte Vetraria*, issued fifty years previously in Italy), and Robert Boyle, the famous chemist.

Meanwhile, the Glass-sellers' Company continued to import stock from Venice, specifying standards of shape, size, and decoration because they knew what their customers would buy. Few examples of the wares shipped to England during this period have survived. However, the letters and accompanying drawings of John Greene, warden of the Glass-sellers' Company, and Alessio Morelli of Venice, preserved in the British Museum, provide knowledge of fashionable glassware between 1667 and 1673. Moreover, the correspondence furnishes information about the business methods of the Company.

Although Venetian suppliers satisfied most of their London clients' demands, including Greene's request that he be "used verj kindlj in the prices," dealing with distant manufacturers created difficulties. Then, too, imported glass was subject to custom duties. As the demand for glassware increased it became obvious to the Company that it would be more profitable to sell a high-quality English glass at a low price than to import. But as yet no one had created the "sound Mettall" needed to produce clear crystal.

Strangely enough, it was not a professional glassmaker who eventually produced the colorless crystal glass desired by the Company. This great technical achievement was accomplished by George Ravenscroft (1618-1681), prosperous merchant, amateur chemist, and close friend of many leading English scientists. The interest of these men in developing an improved glass and Ravenscroft's own experience in handling cargoes of fragile Venetian *cristallo* prompted him to set up an experimental glasshouse in 1673.

One of Ravenscroft's master craftsmen in his London works was Seignior Da Costa of Montferrat who not only instructed his employer in the art of glass blowing but also suggested changes in the traditional English formula for making glass. Following his advice, Ravenscroft used flint crushed from the quartz pebbles found in Italian rivers rather than local sand in the formula and substituted soda containing refined potash from Spain. After eight months of experimentation, Ravenscroft notified the Glass-sellers' Company —which had encouraged his research—that he could furnish them "fine Chrystaline Glasses in semblance of Rock Christall for beer, wine and other uses."

On May 16, 1674, Charles II granted Ravenscroft a seven-year patent on his "fflint-crystalline" which had previously been approved by the Glass-sellers' Company. Not only did the Company agree to buy all of Ravenscroft's output—providing he followed its designs—but also gave him permission to build another glasshouse at Henley-on-Thames where he could experiment in replacing the imported ingredients in his formula with English materials.

The Company had no difficulty in marketing Ravenscroft's clear glassware but was soon swamped with complaints from customers that their

LEFT: *Penruddock flute made in Ravenscroft's Savoy Glasshouse, London, about 1675.*

RIGHT: *Fashioned between 1676 and 1678, this goblet bears the raven's head seal of the Glass-sellers' Company.*

purchases were losing transparency. This defect, known as crizzling, is caused by atmospheric moisture which, absorbed by the surface of the glass, diffuses into the layers below, causing their alkali content to undergo a chemical reaction.

Ravenscroft now had two problems: the overcoming of the divitrification of his glass and the finding of native components for his metal. Working by trial and error, he began replacing the alkali constituent of his formula with lead oxide and, by gradually increasing the amount of lead, eventually evolved a formula that seemingly eliminated crizzling.

Confident that Ravenscroft's improved "fflint glass" overcame the defect of crizzling, the Glass-sellers, through their agents Hawley Bishop and Samuel Moore, assured the public in June of 1676 that "the defect of the flint glasses (which were formerly observed to crissel and decay) hath been redressed." Their statement also contained the first known reference to the characteristic ring of lead crystal, "... ye distinction of sound discernable by any person whatsoever."

To distinguish this glass-of-lead from earlier types, the Company ordered that every article fashioned from it be marked with a seal. The Glass-sellers paid Ravenscroft the compliment of choosing for the identification mark a small glass disc impressed with a raven's head similar to the one borne on his coat of arms. This device was employed by the Company until Ravenscroft's death in 1681. However, very few "sealed" bowls, jugs, and glasses have survived. All of them, despite the guarantee "no crizzling or money returned," are crizzled, for it was not until Hawley Bishop, acting for the Glass-sellers, reduced the silica in Ravenscroft's formula and increased its lead content that crizzling was overcome.

By 1696, twenty-seven English works were producing flint glass, the Company's control of the heaviest, softest, densest, and most brilliant glass yet manufactured having expired in 1681. However, during the early eighteenth century, English glassware owed much to traditional Venetian design, lacked decoration, and was heavy. This last characteristic led to the selling of glass by the pound, as shown in this advertisement in the *Tatler* on August 5, 1710:

> At the flint glasshouse in White Fryars are to be sold all sorts of Decanthers, Drinking Glasses, Crewits, etc., or Glasses made to any pattern, of the best flint at 12d per pound.

But heavy glass disappeared from the glass-sellers' shops before the end of the eighteenth century. Seeking money to finance the wars being waged on the Continent and in the New World, the Crown imposed a series of taxes on glass based on its weight. As a result, glassmakers began fashioning smaller and lighter vessels which were frequently cut or engraved.

Motivated by the Glass Excise Acts of 1745, 1777, and 1787, aided by technical advances, inspired by the revival of classicism in the arts, and out of their own creativeness, English glassmakers slowly developed a distinctly English style of glass. Nothing shows this more graphically than the drinking vessels they fashioned until the craftsman was replaced by machine-molding in 1833.

Antiquarians have determined the chronological order of drinking-glass styles from a wide variety of sources: household inventories, glass-sellers' bills, trade cards, newspaper advertisements, and paintings. Out of this research has come, according to G. Bernard Hughes, the eminent authority on English table glass, "... recognition of six main and twenty-two subsidiary types of stem: these may be further divided according to bowl forms and types of feet."

Little eighteenth-century glassware was the work of independent craftsmen—although a few glassmakers, hoping to avoid taxes, operated clandestine works in rural areas where they produced bottles and jugs. Technical improvements such as Humphrey Perrott's furnace had transformed glassmaking from a handicraft to an industry. However, skilled artisans were employed in every glasshouse to decorate wares with animals, coats-of-arms, epigrams, figures, flowers, geometric patterns, names, toasts, and other designs including those that indicated the beverage for which a glass should be used: bunches of grapes for wine glasses, ears of barley for beer, apple trees for cider.

Although a diamond point had been used to engrave the "eight dishes of glass graven about the rims" made by Verzelini for the Earl of Leicester in 1588, English craftsmen were slow to copy the technique and few diamond-engraved specimens can be definitely attributed to them. In fact, the only diamond-point engraver of whom we have an authenticated record is Giles of York who inscribed a tumbler in 1756.

Nor do we know much about the craftsmen who used an abrasive wheel to engrave glassware with political slogans, representations of historic events, national heroes, hunting scenes, and the ceremonial glasses used by supporters of the House of Stuart when toasting "the King over the water." Incidentally, while the Romans employed the wheel technique—and had introduced it to Britain—the process was forgotten for over a thousand years until Casper Lehmann of Prague revived it about 1590.

Most authorities agree that wheel engraving was reintroduced into England by George Franz Kreybich, a German enameler who settled in London in 1688. Kreybich, Anton Wilhelm Maurel, and other German craftsmen who followed had no competition from native artisans until the close of the

LEFT: *This mammoth Queen Anne goblet stands 16¾" high and is the second largest recorded English goblet in existence. As only one other goblet of similar size would appear to exist today, they must have been extremely rare. It is probable that they were made as fine specimens of early lead glass and belonged to glass-sellers' guilds in some of the prominent glassmaking centers such as London, Bristol, and possibly Newcastle.* CENTER: *Wine bottle of olive green, bubbly glass with the seal of Charles Ludlow.* RIGHT: *"Jacobite" wine glass with copper wheel engraving of the Young Pretender.*

century when certain looking-glass makers began enclosing their mirror plate—which was often engraved—in frames of wheel-engraved glass.

While Sir Robert Mansell had produced the first English-made looking glasses in 1620, Buckingham and later glassmen merely produced mirror plate. "Then," wrote Zacharias Conrad Von Uffenbach, a German student who visited London in 1710, "the panes are sold to other people who cut and mount them, making mirrors of them: this is a special trade followed by many people in London."

Actually, looking glasses were usually the work of two craftsmen: the grinder who ground, polished, and beveled the glass, and the looking-glass maker who did the silvering. The latter process, then known as foiling, consisted of covering the back of the plate with a tin and mercury amalgam, which practice continued until the discovery by Justus von Liebig in 1835 that glass could be coated with a thin film of silver.

Few of the printed labels which looking-glass makers pasted to the backboards of their handiwork have survived. Therefore, unless a bill of sale or other documentation exists, it is impossible to identify the work of individual craftsmen. However, directories and contemporary newspapers reveal the names of many of these artisans, list their specialties, and give the locations of their shops.

49

For example, James Welch, glass grinder and looking-glass maker whose shop was behind *The Rose and Crown* in Blackfriars, informed the public in *The Daily Courant* for July 29, 1724, that:

> You may be furnished Wholesale or Retale with great Variety of Peer, Chimney or Sconce Glasses, fine Dressing-Glasses, Coach, Chariot, or Chair-Glasses with Plate Sash-Glasses, &c.
> N.B. Merchants, Shop-keepers, or Country Chapmen may be furnished with the aforementioned Goods, as also all sorts of small Glasses at the Lowest Rates. Old Glasses cleaned or made into new Fashions.

After mastering the technique of engraving mirrors and their frames, a number of craftsmen began decorating tableware. None were more skilled than Joseph Martin, Benjamin Payne, and Jerom Johnson, the first glass-seller in London to describe himself as "Glass Engraver." While Martin worked for the Fitzsimmons glasshouse in Dublin and both Payne and Johnson owned shops, most eighteenth-century glass engravers plied their craft in their homes. Using a foot-operated lathe to turn wheels which were coated with emery powder of varying degrees of coarseness and linseed oil, they engraved original designs, patterns dictated by customers, or copied artists' sketches. When the engraving was intricate, the design was outlined on the glass with white paint applied with a quill, but simple patterns were freehand engraved.

In the late 1750's, glass-sellers added engravers to their staffs, but the day of the independent artisan was not over. Even in 1777 engravers were seeking commissions, as did Thomas Billinge whose notice in the *Liverpool Advertiser* stated that he was "a glass flowerer cutting patterns representing flowers on vases and other domestic glassware."

"Flowered glass"—the trade name for vessels decorated with flowers on the bowl—was not difficult to engrave. Thousands of pieces bearing flowers, festoons, and geometric patterns were supplied to glass merchants by middlemen who purchased tableware from glasshouses and hired dozens of engravers to cover it with standard patterns. However, engraving coats of arms remained the province of the independent craftsman because such work required the highest skill and extreme accuracy.

Although the Romans were masters of the art of cutting glass, the technique had been forgotten for centuries. Like wheel engraving, it was revived by Caspar Lehmann, who, in 1609, was appointed glass cutter to the Court of Emperor Rudolf II. German craftsmen soon became adept at decorating glass by cutting it in patterns and thus enhancing its refractive power, but English artisans of the seventeenth century showed little interest in the process.

*Magnificent Chinese mirror-picture in English giltwood frame, by Thomas Chippendale, 1765.*

Left: *Chippendale carved and gilded overmantel landscape mirror surmounted by an oil painting of sporting birds.* Right: *"Glass flowerers"—craftsmen who specialized in cutting floral patterns—were active in the late 18th century.*

Nevertheless, a few London grinders of the period adopted the revived technique. Richard Robinson, inventor of a grinding machine "worked by wheels and water," advertised frequently during 1698 that his stock at *The Flower Pot* included "looking-glass plates—the Borders cut more curiously Hollow and with a better lustre than any heretofore done."

However, little table glass was cut in England until John Akerman, a leading London glass-seller, hired German workmen early in the eighteenth century. Akerman also employed expert native glass grinders but they only scalloped the tops of bowls or cut the thickest parts of a piece because of their lack of experience. By the time glass cutting was a specialized craft in England, technical improvements had brought about the production of a flint glass of greater toughness and refractive power.

Using this metal and their newly acquired skill, English glass cutters eventually became recognized as the finest in the world. By means of flat, round, and V-shaped edged wheels of varying sizes, they placed ornamental motifs on vessels of all kinds. This was no easy task even if the cutter used the underside of the wheel—as did glass engravers—while decorating the

LEFT: *One of a pair of free-blown and cut candlesticks, about 1760.* RIGHT: *Typical of Anglo-Irish glass of the late 18th century, this sweetmeet glass is free-blown and cut.*

outside of a ware. Far more difficult was the technique used by the majority of cutters. They worked with the top of the wheel. As a result, they had to look down through the glass while creating their patterns on it from below.

Until 1835 when the steam-driven glass-cutting mill came into general use, cutting wheels were turned by an apprentice in the homes of artisans commissioned by glass-sellers. Then, as a new design became increasingly popular, as many as fifty craftsmen might be employed in producing it in an establishment that supplied the trade with stock patterns.

Other glass merchants besides Akerman employed their own cutters. Among these was Thomas Betts who had learned the arts of engraving and cutting glass from Andrew Pawl of Germany, one of his employees. Betts, who established the *King's Arm Glass Shop* at Charing Cross about 1730, was creator of the spire-finialed stopper for decanters, a specialist in "curious work in Looking-glasses," and a proud craftsman whose trade card stated that he was a "Real Workman."

While Betts did much to develop English cut glass, far more was accomplished by his contemporary Jerom Johnson of the *Intire Glass Shop* in the Strand where both china and glass were sold. A self-taught cutter, Johnson not only devised designs for English tables but also special patterns for export. An outstanding businessman as well as a creative artist, Johnson was the first cutter to insert notices in newspapers. In the *London Evening Post* for February 19, 1751 he offered the public:

... all sorts of fine Flint Glasses, brilliant lustres, Branches, Candlesticks, Dishes, Plates, Bowls, Basons, Cups and Covers, Saucers, Salt Cellars, Rummers cut and flowered, Desart Glasses scallop'd or engrav'd, Salvers, large Glasses for cool Tankards, Cruets and Castors, curious Lamps, Wash-hand Glasses most curiously engrav'd new fashion'd or scallop'd, and finest polish'd mugs and Pitchers, Turkish fashion'd Diamond cut and Brilliant Polished; wholesale and retail at the most reasonable rates, and to be sure no where cheaper in London, being the first inventor, Jerom Johnson.

Johnson's advertisement makes it plain that British craftsmen produced a wide variety of glass objects during the eighteenth century. Some, such as bottles, had been made since the days of the Romans; others were recent innovations. Among the latter were chandeliers, the first English reference to these being in 1714 when John Gumley, the London looking-glass maker, advertised in the *London Gazette* that he sold "Glass Schandeliers."

Among the other leading chandelier designers were W. Turing and William Parker. The latter was glassmaker to the Prince of Wales and his trade card, printed in 1770, shows thirty-two glass pieces, half of which are for

*Chandelier of cut glass and ormolu in the Adam taste, about 1790.*

*A rare pair of candelabra on white and green marble bases.*

providing some form of illumination. Thomas Betts also ground glass drops for chandeliers. Originally, these were known as lustres, a term later expanded to mean chandelier as shown by Jerom Johnson's 1739 announcement in the *Daily Post*: " . . . Likewise to be sold cheap the most magnificent lustre made in England."

Chandeliers were also made by Irish craftsmen, but London was the center of their manufacture. The capital city also continued to dictate the form and ornamentation of tableware as it had since Verzelini's day. However, artisans elsewhere—such as the father-and-son team of Samuel and John Callinge of Newcastle, where glass had been made since the seventh century—produced outstanding work. Nevertheless, Newcastle is more famous for the crown glass and bottles made at the works operated by the three Dagnia brothers and their successors than for the flint tableware the Callinges decorated for the local market.

Even more renowned are the wares made in and about Stourbridge. The first glasshouse in the district—which is still a glassmaking center—had been established about 1610 by Paul Tyzack, a Lorrainer. Stourbridge glassmen made colored, cut, and enameled glass as well as bottles, panes, and tableware.

Stourbridge also supplied Victorian whatnots with a wide variety of art glass. Benjamin Richardson, one of three glassmaking brothers associated with Stourbridge glassworks, developed pearl satin glass and a method of providing cameo relief designs on a cased glass blank. The Richardsons were probably the first to make glass paperweights in England, but the honor of producing the first millefiori weight (consisting of brilliantly hued florets cut from colored glass rods resting on a base of clear or latticino

*Webb-cameo glass vase.*

*Wine glass, free-blown, cut, and engraved. Attributed to Apsley Pellatt.*

glass) is credited to Apsley Pellatt, owner of the Falcon Glassworks in London. Besides this accomplishment, Pellatt patented a method, known as Crystallo-Ceramie, of enclosing medallions of pottery or other material in glass, wrote two books on glassmaking, and invented a device for closing molds.

Among the craftsmen using Benjamin Richardson's cameo-glass technique was Joseph Locke, who migrated to America where he produced various types of art glass including Amberina, Pomona, and Agata for the New England Glass Company. But the artisan who profited the most from Richardson's knowledge was his onetime apprentice, John Northwood. An outstanding craftsman, Northwood, after three years of work, in 1876 completed a reproduction of the famous Portland Vase—a glass tomb-vase made in the third century A.D. He also carved the Pegasus Vase now on display in the Smithsonian Institution in Washington, D.C., which depicts stories from Greek and Roman mythology—a task that took six years.

Northwood trained a great number of apprentices. Some eventually became the most famous glassmen of the nineteenth century: John Northwood, II (his son), William and Charles Northwood (his nephews), George and Thomas Woodall, W. O. Bowen, James Hill, B. Fenn, Frederick Carder (who later headed the Steuben Glass Works in America), and Joshua Hogetts who "invariably had in front of him while he worked a specimen of the subject he was engraving, whether flowers, fruit or plant."

About the middle of the eighteenth century, brilliantly decorated porcelains from the Far East became very fashionable in England. To meet this competition, British glassmen began manufacturing opaque glass that had the appearance of porcelain.

The first known advertisement for this new product appeared in the *Bristol Journal* in 1764 and, within a short time, Bristol was famous for its milky white glass. While a great deal of it was fired just enough to fix the gold that decorated it, a far greater amount was ornamented by the transfer process—similar to modern-day use of decals. However, the most permanent and attractive designs were painted in bright colors.

This work was done by free-lance artists who boldly copied the patterns, flowers, birds, and figures of the Oriental artisans who decorated the imported porcelains. One favorite motif was that of the "Long Elizas"—attenuated Chinese ladies carrying parasols—imitations of the *mei-yen* or "graceful ladies" of Cantonese painters. The origin of the term "Long Elizas" stems from the inability of the Dutch merchants who originally controlled the Far Eastern trade to pronounce *mei-yen*. They called the tall beauties *lange lijsen* (long stupids) and this in turn was corrupted into

LEFT: *South Staffordshire opaque baluster vase, about 1765.* RIGHT: *Pepper pot of opaque white glass with enamel decorations, probably Bristol.*

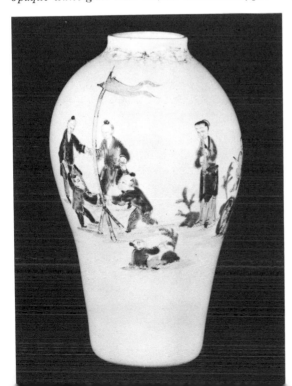

*Pair of early Adam candelabra on blue Bristol glass bases with ormolu mounts.*

"Long Elizas" by English seamen.

There is little doubt that certain Bristol vases, scent bottles, snuff boxes, candlesticks, and tea caddies were enameled by the same artists who painted Worcester porcelain with English birds and flowers, for there is a similarity in style in the two ornamentations. Most of these craftsmen went from pottery to glasshouse seeking work, and are unknown. Others bought vessels "in the white" from Jacob Little's White Flint Glasshouse, John Perrot, or the Redcliffe Backs Glasshouse and, after decorating them, sold them to merchants.

We know little about these painters. For example, six tea caddies are attributed to Michael Edkins, yet his ledger shows he decorated only one. Moreover, while London's Victoria and Albert Museum owns candlesticks and cruets supposedly decorated by Edkins, there is no evidence that he did the work. Actually, the whereabouts of most pieces painted by Edkins is unknown although he did invoice about 350 items between 1762 and 1767. But one authority wryly comments that "the number of so-called Michael Edkins pieces in the United States of America vastly exceeds this."

However, we do know that Edkins came to Bristol about 1760 where he painted post chaises with "handsome gold ornaments, cyphers and crests" and delftware with equal skill. Eventually, he opened his own shop, mar-

58

ried, and fathered thirty-three children. When not painting or watching his muffle furnace, Edkins—who had an excellent counter tenor—sang on Bristol and London stages. He also played small parts and sang the solo songs in the plays whenever touring Shakespearean companies visited Bristol.

In addition to enameled opaque glass, Bristol also produced a radiant blue flint glass. The secret of its manufacture was cobalt, first discovered in Saxony, a region once rich in valuable minerals. The Saxons believed that these minerals were guarded by kobalds (gnomes) and, when the veins petered out in the sixteenth century, blamed these supernatural creatures for transforming precious ore into a substance which became known as cobalt. Long considered worthless, cobalt became an important export when glassmakers discovered it was an excellent source of blue pigments.

Using Saxon cobalt, Bristol glassmakers manufactured a beautiful dark blue glass. Frequently, it was decorated with gold. Edkins is known to have done some of this work, as is his fellow Bristol craftsman Isaac Jacobs, who inscribed his gilded tableware "I. Jacobs."

While Edkins was decorating in Bristol, the most famous enamel painters of the eighteenth century were working in Newcastle. They were William Beilby (1740-1819) and his sister Mary (1749-1787). Gifted members of a talented family—their father William Beilby, Sr., was a silversmith while their brother Ralph Beilby was a renowned heraldic engraver—the two were outstanding craftsmen. Using a cool, bluish-white enamel, they decorated drinking vessels with birds, butterflies, flowers, landscapes, and waving foli-

The only known pair of signed Beilby goblets. Note the rendering of the leaf sprays under the crest, also the scrolled leaves that flank the crown of arms. Both are characteristic Beilby treatment.

LEFT: *Early 19th-century Nailsea olive green bowl with spatters of white and colored glass.* RIGHT: *Cobalt blue sugar bowl, pattern molded, about 1780.*

age. They also produced rococo scrollwork and commemorative designs for special occasions.

Just as Bristol has given its name to all dark blue English glass, the glasshouses at Nailsea, seven miles away, are credited with objects made in Sunderland, Newcastle, Scotland, and elsewhere. But no matter where so-called Nailsea was made, it reveals the English glassmaker in his most festive mood.

Generally speaking, Nailsea is a generic term for a variety of objects made of both opaque and translucent glass of many different colors, gaily patterned with contrasting loops, spots, splashes, and waves of a contrasting hue. Nailsea wares include such fripperies as coaching horns, glass bells, huge tobacco pipes, mantel ornaments, paperweights, shepherds' crooks, wall decorations, walking sticks, witch balls, "fairings," and various shaped flasks such as the gimmel which has two spouts.

Nailsea is supposedly the source of all the glass rolling pins made in England (many of which are reproductions) which originally were designed as airtight salt boxes, but later, after being lavishly decorated and filled with sweets, were treasured as love tokens. They also served as good luck charms, being hung beside the hearth to keep out evil spirits, and were, tradition has it, often used to smuggle tea and brandy through customs. This well may be true, but many of the pins were obviously made for the prosaic task of rolling dough, for their only opening is a tiny hole to provide for the expansion and contraction of the glass.

The majority of Englishmen could not afford engraved, cut, or enameled glassware. Nevertheless, from Ravenscroft's day to 1864 when William Leighton developed an inexpensive lime-glass that made large-scale commercial molding and pressing of glass possible, surface-decorated glassware has graced British tables.

Eighteenth-century glassmen often impressed a pattern on glass with a mold, then withdrew the hot metal and expanded it—a process which had no effect on the design except to enlarge it. They also used hand-operated pinchers in which dies were set to shape solid units such as candlestick parts and decanter stoppers, and "pinching" became a recognized craft. By the mid-1790's, shallow tableware was being formed by the use of a hand press but it was not until the nineteenth century when the blown-mold technique was perfected that tableware was mass-produced.

The decline of handcraftmanship began in 1802 when Charles Chubsbee invented the two-piece mold. A Stourbridge glassblower, Chubsbee lacked the funds to patent his device, which permitted reproduction of the shapes and designs of handblown, handcut, glass. By 1825, four-piece molds were in use but the wares blown in them were marred with tool and mold marks. This defect was overcome in the 1820's when the process of fire-polishing glassware came into general use.

Meanwhile, Deming Jarves and Enoch Robinson were arguing in American courts over their respective rights to a patent for a glass-pressing machine. Both claimed to have invented identical devices: molten glass was

*Bristol scent bottle of blue glass with enamel and gilt decoration.*

*A group of Bristol and Nailsea wares: a "Remember Me" cup; an enameled vase; a glass rolling pin; a candy-cane perfume bottle; and a souvenir cup.*

poured into a mold, pressed down with a plunger, and allowed to cool and harden. Then the mold was opened and the ware removed.

The first glass-pressing machine was installed in England at Stourbridge by W. H. P. Richardson in 1833 and within a few months machines were in operation in most glasshouses. There was good reason. Faulty patent laws made reproduction of the American device possible without payment of royalties. Glassmakers began producing a wide variety of pressed glass from stock molds or patterns of their own design—the quality of the vessel depending on the care with which the mold had been fashioned, the care given it, the skill of the pressers, and the polishing given the finished article.

Although glass-pressing machines eliminated the need for highly skilled craftsmen, creative artisans continued to cut glass. However, most cut glass of the Victorian period is far below the standard of earlier days. The repeal of the excise tax on glass in 1845 allowed English glassmen to make their vessels as heavy as they wished and, the thicker they were, the more profusely they could be cut. Ugly in form—vessels being given only shapes that permitted the most extravagant cutting—Victorian cut glass shows that the English glassmaker was "quite incapable of profiting by his artistic freedom."

The Great Exhibition of the Industry of all Nations held in Hyde Park in 1851 provides proof of the decline in English glassmaking. However, the

Crystal Palace which housed the Exhibition was a bold, new, and exciting use of glass. It was designed by Joseph Paxton, the first European to bring *Victoria regina*, a lily from equatorial Africa, into bloom in a conservatory. Paxton was also responsible for improvements in greenhouse construction, including the manufacture of larger and clearer panes of glass.

But the Crystal Palace was his greatest achievement. The forerunner of modern-day prefabricated structures and the first demountable building, Paxton's masterpiece was 1,851 feet long (the largest edifice erected up to that time) and covered eighteen acres. Its central section was vaulted with a semicircular glass dome, while its two long wings, roofed in three mounting levels, resembled wedding-cake tiers. Paxton ordered the 900,000 square feet of glass needed to enclose the iron girders that formed the Palace's skeleton from the Chance brothers in Birmingham who had assisted him in his experiments with greenhouse sash.

While the vast majority of the six million people who visited the Exhibition during the twenty-four weeks it remained open gaped with astonishment at the sights, most of the glass on display brought nothing but criticism from those who had hoped to find a fusion of the arts and the machine. There was good reason: "The glassware exhibited was for the most part

*These glasses made to celebrate Victoria's Jubilee have coins in their stems.*

*Cameo plate—an overlay of white over puce glass—carved by George Woodall in the 1890's.*

fantastically over-elaborate, showing an entirely mistaken belief in the value of applied ornament, and a misguided stress on size."

None found more fault with the poorly designed and extravagantly decorated glass shown at the Crystal Palace than artist William Morris, who advocated simplicity of form and decoration. Therefore, Morris (who was responsible for an international revival in arts and crafts) commissioned Philip Webb, an architect, to design a drinking-glass service that had these attributes. Morris then had the glasses made in London by the Whitefriar's Glassworks operated by James Powell, whose family had founded the business in 1680.

Morris could not have made a better choice. Powell was a student of glassmaking and an inventor of new techniques of glass decoration. His son Harry J. Powell was also a skilled glassman and, in 1864, was chosen by Morris to create the glasses designed for him by Sir Thomas Jackson, another architect. Between 1880 and 1920 the Whitefriar's Glassworks was the source of some of the most attractive glass made in England, designed by Barnaby Powell, Tom Hill, and James Hogan.

Similarly, other designers including Graham Sunderland, Eric Ravilious, and Clyne Farquharson have created contemporary glass for various firms, most of which was mass-produced. However, as a general rule, English glassworks maintain a special department for the production of unique items or for "limited editions" of high artistic merit.

Such glass is the work of relatively young artist-craftsmen. Among this group are Laurence Whistler and Jane Webster, master of the art of glass engraving. Many of these young people have attended one of the following schools: Stourbridge Academy, supported by the glassmakers of that city, the University of Sheffield, noted for glass technology research; or the Royal College of Art in London, which offers a three-year course in glass designing and decorating.

Unfortunately, despite their training, few graduates of these institutions have the ability to blow glass. Therefore, certain glasshouses run glass-blowing schools. As a result, it well may be that, in time, the present system of a skilled craftsman's fashioning a ware from someone else's design will vanish and English glass will once again be produced by artist-artisans who have a complete understanding and mastery of the material with which they work.

# 3

## *Pottery and Porcelain*

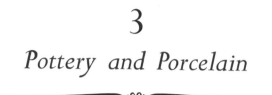

Potters have practiced their craft in England since Neolithic man first discovered that moist clay could be molded and then fixed into permanent form by exposure to heat. However, the craft made little progress until the Roman occupation, when the island's conquerors imported Continental potters to work native clays. These craftsmen were not only adept in using their fingers to raise a variety of forms from the clay they threw on the potter's wheel but also employed the lathe to finish their creations which they often glazed and frequently decorated.

Native artisans soon acquired these techniques, only to forget them when the German tribes overran England following the withdrawal of the legions at the beginning of the fifth century. In fact, the funerary urns—which represent almost all known pottery made in Anglo-Saxon Britain—are of no better quality than the wares made in pre-Roman times.

Nor did the English potters of medieval times display much skill. Their vessels, molded from coarse, unrefined red, buff, or gray clays, covered with a translucent lead glaze colored green, yellow, or purplish-black, were rude, poorly fired, and rarely ornamented. The only exception were the tiles fashioned by Cistercian monks. Working with the same materials as the village potmaker, these craftsmen, using secret techniques and their native talent, manufactured sturdy tiles to pave the floors and walls of churches, inlaying their handiwork with various designs.

Although the dissolution of the monasteries by Henry VIII in 1540 put out the fires in abbey kilns, the art of potting advanced under the Tudors. Vessels of metal and horn were replaced by "pottes" and decorated tableware came into use. While much of this pottery was made by native artisans, they had to compete with the "drinking stone pottes" made in Cologne and the stove tiles and tableware imported from the Low Countries.

The last named were gaily decorated, their smooth white surfaces—achieved by adding oxide of tin to the lead glaze—being easily painted. "Gally paving tiles" and other "mailolica" tin-glazed ware were first made

LEFT: *English earthenware jug, 13th to 15th century.* RIGHT: *An example of "mailolica" or tin-glazed earthenware, 1697.*

in England by Gaspar Andries and Guy Janson, who left their native Antwerp to avoid religious persecution, settled in Norwich, and, in 1570, began potting "after the fashion used in Flanders."

Shortly thereafter the two moved to London, petitioning Elizabeth I that they "might have Liberty to follow their trade in that City without interruption." Whether Andries, Janson, or one of the other Flemish potters who joined them fashioned the surviving painted pottery dishes, drug jars, and other vessels of this period is unknown, for similar wares were shipped into England by Guido Andries—a relation to Gaspar—from the Netherlands.

But there is no doubt that the majority of mugs and jugs in which English innkeepers of the sixteenth century served ale were "potts made at Cullein." Thousands of these pots were imported from Cologne and other Continental pottery centers specializing in the manufacture of stoneware—a partially vitrified pottery that is impervious to liquids, acid resistant, and more or less translucent when thin.

German-made stoneware flagons, jugs, pots, and pitchers were glazed with salt, Rhenish potters having discovered that throwing salt through holes in the top of a kiln when the ware was red hot coated it with a fine, very hard, glossy glaze. Both attractive and durable, this imported salt-

67

LEFT: *In all ages English potters have expressed their sense of humor in clay.* RIGHT: *Strong but delicate hands and years of experience go into this man's ability to create beauty out of a handful of clay on a potter's wheel.*

glazed stoneware gave native pottery so much competition that English craftsmen sought to duplicate it early in the seventeenth century. Thomas Rous and Abraham Cullen received a patent from Charles I in 1626 to make the pottery "comonly called or knowne by the name or names of stone potte, stone jugge, and stone bottelle."

Whether these men actually made salt-glazed stoneware is unknown. If they did, they could not have been successful because in 1635—five years before the expiration of their patent—a group headed by David Ramsey received sole rights to manufacture "Earthen Comodityes within this our Realme which nowe are made by Straungers in Forraigne Partes."

What ware Ramsey and his associates produced and where they had their pottery—if they had one—is a mystery. So are the names of the artisans who made the salt-glazed "wasters"—discarded pottery which provides evidence of the existence of a kiln in the place where they are found—unearthed in and around London. These wasters are similar to the "graybeards"—bulbous pots whose necks bear the harsh features of a bearded man —known to be made on the Continent. Such pots are also known as Bellarmines, tradition holding that they represent the unpopular Cardinal Bellarmine who was caricatured in clay by Low Country potters after his death in 1621. Incidentally, Bellarmines are the source of the slang expression "mug" used in reference to the human face.

It is possible that the earliest salt-glazed English stoneware were experimental pieces made by John Dwight (1640?-1703) before he applied to Charles II for a patent in 1671. In his petition, Dwight claimed that he had discovered "The Mistery of Transparent Earthenware, Comonly Knowne by the Names of Porcelaine or China, and Persian Ware, as Alsoe the Misterie of the Stone Ware Vulgarly called Cologne Ware."

Dwight was no ordinary potter. A graduate of Oxford, an ecclesiastical lawyer, and sometime secretary to the Bishop of Chester, he was a student of the arts and sciences. He also may have been a talented sculptor because his figurines and busts are "undoubtedly the finest and most original productions of any English potter." However, it is unknown if Dwight modeled these pieces.

Some time before Dwight applied for an extension of his original patent in 1684, he established a pottery at Fulham, then a village just outside London. During Dwight's lifetime, its kilns produced a wide variety of wares: a dinner set for Charles II; marbled, blue, and mouse-colored tablewares; deep bronze or white statuettes of classical and contemporary figures; and various vessels of a whitish, salt glazed stoneware. Thanks to Dwight's business acumen, this stoneware replaced that imported from the Continent. He turned his entire output over to the Glass-sellers' Company under a contract that stipulated that the Company would not sell foreign ware.

Dwight may have been a clever businessman but he was a most eccentric character. While he carefully recorded in notebooks the results of forty years of experimentation with various clays, he had the habit of burying his memoranda. Dwight also had a mania for hiding money in various places, noting its location in a ledger, then crossing out the entry when he removed the money. Typical of his "banking" is this deposit and withdrawal:

1693  9ber
In ye garret in a hole under ye fireplace 240 G in a wooden box.

His passion for hiding things evidently included stoneware. When the original factory at Fulham was demolished in 1689, a vault was unearthed which contained a number of his creations. These wares provide proof that Dwight had indeed solved "the mysterie of the Cologne wares." However, we have no clue as to where he buried or secreted the special tools, molds, and models used to fashion such fine wares as his figurines.

Certain authorities maintain that Dwight concealed these articles because he did not want his family—who operated the pottery until 1746 when it passed into other hands—to reproduce his masterpieces. Others hold that Dwight's action stemmed from his desire to prevent his son and widow from continuing the least remunerative branch of the business. Still others feel that Dwight, frustrated in his attempts to create true porcelain, deliberately omitted recording where he buried certain tools and formulas in order to remove the temptation of continuing his experiments.

Dwight had good reason to be disgruntled over his failure to compound porcelain. Despite years of work and the expenditure of large sums of money, he had failed to produce a ware comparable to the translucent Oriental vessels wealthy Englishmen proudly displayed along with ostrich eggs and cocoanut shells mounted in silver. Royalty as well as rich commoners had been collecting porcelain avidly for years—no present Elizabeth I received as a New Year's gift in 1587 pleased her more than the "porrynger of white porselyn, garnished with gold, the cover of gold, with a lyon on the toppe thereof" given to her by Lord William Cecil.

But the master potter of Fulham never benefited from the ever-increasing demand for porcelain. Successful in the manufacture of stoneware, he was frustrated in his lifelong effort to learn the secret of the formula of Oriental ware.

Meanwhile, country potters and London-based craftsmen were fashioning products for sale at fairs and in city shops. They also potted vessels ordered to celebrate special occasions or for gifts: tygs (many-handled loving cups); fuddling cups (formed by joining together several cups open at the bottom which made draining a single cup impossible); jugs in the form of owls; and puzzle jugs. The latter had several perforations in the neck and a number of spouts and drenched all who tilted them except those experienced in their use. The secret was to use one's fingers to close the hidden hole under the handle and all the spouts save the one that enabled the liquid to be removed by suction.

As the sixteenth century drew to a close, most potters ornamented their ware with slip—clay of a creamy consistency. This technique, known since the Roman occupation, was revived by foreign craftsmen who settled in Kent in 1582 and retaught it to local artisans at Wrotham. English potters used slip in various ways: as a wash to hide the color of the body (if the surface was then combed with a toothed tool a marble effect was achieved);

LEFT: *A fuddling cup of tin-enameled earthenware, 1650. Joining the bottoms of the jugs made it impossible to empty one.* RIGHT: *A Liverpool puzzle jug. If the unwary drinker did not close all the openings with his fingers, he was drenched.*

to create patterns dotted or trailed on the surface from a sprouted vessel; for barbotine designs (low reliefs molded from a slip paste); and in the sgraffito process (coating a ware with slip of contrasting color, then scratching a design through to the underlying clay).

While potters catering to the Puritan trade sparsely ornamented their ware and inscribed it by hand with such pious warnings as "Remember God," others, including John Meir of the Cockpit Hill Pottery in Derby, employed molds to form barbotine decorations. Still others, particularly Staffordshire clay workers, preferred to use the slip-pot to trace their ornamentation.

The large, deep, flat-based, broad-rimmed dishes, dating from the seventeenth century on, are typical of Staffordshire slip ware. After covering the body, formed from coarse reddish or buff-colored clay, with white slip, the potter outlined a design in brown slip, then filled it in, embellishing the rim of the dish with contrasting colors.

Because certain examples of these dishes bear the name of Thomas Toft, they are known as Toft ware. Thomas and his brother Ralph operated a pottery near Shelton where they fashioned crude wares decorated with great skill. Their freehand technique and patterns were copied by others,

71

but it is impossible to determine if Ralph Turnor, Robert Shaw, George or William Taylor—whose names along with others appear on Staffordshire slip-decorated dishes—were the makers or receivers of these surviving wares.

Unlike slip ware which became a purely British product, English delft owes everything—including its name—to foreign influence. First made about 1600 in Delft, Holland, by Dutch potters seeking to compete with the blue-and-white china being imported from the Orient, the secret of its manufacture was carried across the Channel thirty years later by immigrant craftsmen who settled in Lambeth.

Eventually, there were twenty delft works in this section of London but, although Lambeth potteries—and those that made delft elsewhere in England—used the same process as Dutch craftsmen, they never created ware equal to that of Holland. Not only was the body of Dutch delft softer, its glaze was thicker and more lustrous, its decoration more artistic. Moreover, the English glaze was prone to crack or craze, while its blue coloring had a gray tone.

Protected by a Royal Proclamation forbidding the importation of "coloured earthenware," Lambeth potters dipped their brushes into a wide variety of shades to decorate delft in a diversity of designs. Some surviving examples of their work have borders consisting of slanting blue strokes—the so-called "blue-dash chargers"—while others bear such quaint inscriptions as "Drink To Thy Friend Bvt Remember Thy Ende."

Early in the eighteenth century, Lambeth delft had to compete with that made in Bristol and Liverpool. The most celebrated Bristol delft consists of

LEFT: *A "blue-dash charger," probably representing William III. Note the slanting dashes around the edge. Late 17th century.* CENTER: *Bristol delft Adam and Eve charger, about 1720.* RIGHT: *An 18th-century Bristol delft dish decorated by Michael Edkins.*

*Like their fellow craftsmen in Liverpool, Staffordshire potters decorated wares with marine scenes by transfer printing.*

pieces ornamented with designs in white enamel—the only English delft so decorated. This white on white ware is known to collectors as *bianco sopra bianco*.

Actually, Bristol had but two delft works in the eighteenth century. One was owned by Joseph Flower, the other by Richard Frank. The latter employed, among other painters, John Hope, Thomas Patience, and Michael Edkins, the famous enameler of Bristol blue glass.

Meanwhile, nearly twenty delft works were operating in Liverpool. Alderman Shaw was probably the first Liverpool potter to make delft. While the earliest known example of his work is dated 1716, its quality suggests that Shaw had considerable previous experience. Richard Chaffers, an apprentice of Shaw, profited greatly by his master's knowledge, for the delft he produced in the pottery he established about 1752 was among the best of its time, much of it being exported to the American colonies.

Liverpool delft punch bowls are outstanding examples of the potter's art. Many bear the representation of a particular vessel, having been designed for the use of those who toasted a ship before its departure or to celebrate its return. The finest of these bowls were made by Seth Pennington, one of three brothers, each of whom operated his own pottery. Seth, the most talented of the trio, fashioned delft of a rich blue hue.

While Seth Pennington made various wares, Zachariah Barnes specialized in delft. He is best known for his tiles. Usually, their ornamentation of flowers, scenes, and figures was in blue, but Barnes used other colors as well. He also employed overglaze transfer printing to decorate his work.

The process of transferring imprints from a copper plate to an enameled or glazed surface was the joint invention of Stephen Theodore Janssen, a London stationer; John Brooks, a mezzotint engraver; and Henry Delamain, an Irish delft potter. In 1753, this trio formed a company to decorate the

73

snuff boxes and other small articles made at the Battersea enamel works owned by Janssen. When the company failed three years later, Janssen was declared bankrupt and his stock sold at auction. John Sadler, a Liverpool engraver, attended the sale and acquired enough material to enable him and his partner Guy Green to establish themselves as transfer printers.

In addition to ornamenting wares for local potters, Sadler and Green did a great deal of work for distant manufacturers who found—as did Josiah Wedgwood—that it was cheaper to ship their products to Liverpool to be decorated by transfer printing than to have them painted locally by hand.

It was typical of Wedgwood and his fellow Staffordshire potters to send their wares to Liverpool to cut costs. No workers in clay were more enterprising than those of the Potteries (the place name given to Tunsall, Burslem, Hanley, Stoke, and Longton) and to the communities surrounding the "Five Towns." Out of the inventive genius, artistic skill, and business ability of the inhabitants, a peasant art developed into an industry that still flourishes.

The craft of potting must have been established in Staffordshire at a very early date because a manor list for 1299 records a Robert le Pottere, Thomas Potinger, and Richard Throware. However, although mid-seventeenth century court records and tax rolls contain the names of many potters, little is known of these men, many of whom worked at the same time as the Toft brothers.

Cut off from London by distance and poor roads, the peasant potters of Staffordshire had little knowledge of the techniques and formulas introduced by foreign craftsmen. Working in shops attached to their homes, they formed all their clay by hand with the exception of "spriggs"—raised decorations on small pieces—which they molded; they had no knowledge of enamel painting until after 1750; nor did they use a lathe to smooth the plain, marbled, and slip-decorated tableware, various sized bottles, puzzle jugs, tygs, miniature cradles (given by local custom to newly married couples), and butter pots that came from their kilns. Most of the latter were shipped to Uttoxeter in west-central Staffordshire, site of a great dairy produce market, while the other wares were sold to peddlers who carried them "at their backs all over the whole Countrey"

Although Charles II had granted John Dwight "the sole use and benefitt of an Invencon" for making stoneware, Staffordshire potters infringed upon his patent. Therefore, he brought suit against John Elers, David Elers, Aaron Wedgwood, Thomas Wedgwood, Richard Wedgwood, Matthew Garner, James Morley, and John Chandler.

The Elers brothers were "forreigners and by trade silversmiths" who, after learning to make stoneware in Cologne, settled in Fulham when

*Miniature cradle made as a christening gift by a Staffordshire potter.*

William of Orange assumed the English throne in 1669. Dwight claimed that they had acquired the formula for the body of their "redd thea potts" from his former employee John Chandler, in order to profit from the increased demand for tea services.

While the Elers managed to affect a settlement out of court, Dwight secured injunctions against the other defendants. The court also decided in his favor in another suit brought against Cornelius Hammersley, Moses Middleton, and Joshua Astbury of Staffordshire in 1697. By then the Wedgwoods had also arranged a compromise settlement which probably consisted of each party paying its own costs, for the record shows that Dwight sued his solicitor for charging excessive fees.

The Elers may have stolen Dwight's formula—although they denied even knowing Chandler—but they could not contradict Dwight's charge that they were benefiting from the growing use of tea. Originally considered a medicine—Thomas Garway, England's first tea merchant, advertised the beverage in 1660 as a means of "preserving perfect health until extreme Old Age"—tea had become Britain's national drink. As a result, there was a ready market for well-made tea pots, and the Elers, using a Chinese type as a model, fashioned excellent ones from Staffordshire clay supplied by the Wedgwoods.

Shortly after making their settlement with Dwight, the Elers closed their Fulham pottery. While John remained in London, David went to Bradwell Wood in Staffordshire where he made "red porcelaine" wares identical to those manufactured by Dwight. There was little in common between this hard red stoneware with its thin, light, smooth body and artistic decoration and the other ware of the region. Whether David Elers was responsible for the technique of ornamenting pottery by fixing a soft piece of clay on it

*A glazed earthenware Staffordshire coffeepot, Astbury type, about 1745.*

*A group of early Staffordshire mantel ornaments.*

with a metal seal is a debatable question—but no one did such work with more skill. Elers did not glaze his products—all of which reflect "the hand of the ex-silversmith in size, shape and finish"—but fired them at such high temperatures that they were extremely solid.

In order to keep others from copying his techniques, Elers laid earthenware voice pipes throughout his factory which enabled him to warn of the approach of visitors; transported his wares only at night; and is reputed to have locked up his workmen during the day and subjected them to a search before they left the premises. Therefore, he was delighted when two men of obviously low mentality applied for work—there was little danger of their learning his secrets. He was wrong. The pair—John Astbury and Joshua Twyford—were no fools but were merely feigning stupidity to gain admittance to the pottery. They soon acquired knowledge of Elers' processes and, when their employer who had never been happy in Staffordshire returned to London in 1710, opened their own works.

It was no easy task for John Astbury (c. 1678-1743) to give the impression of imbecility. He had a keen mind, outstanding artistic skill, and a strong desire to improve the art of potting. Working with Twyford, he produced wares similar to those made by Elers. However, when their partnership was dissolved, he developed new bodies and designs. Astbury also improved the salt-glaze process and imported clay from Devonshire—to which he added powdered flint, enabling him to make a whiter body than his neighbors.

Although not trained as a sculptor, Astbury was the first Staffordshire potter to make figures. He fashioned excellent ceramic representations of animals, birds, and humans, as did his son Thomas in his own pottery at Lane Delph. However, the Astbury family had no monopoly on artistic skill, nor were their formulas protected by patents. Other potters duplicated their wares—the Malkins, Shaws, Simpsons, Taylors, Woods, Wedgwoods, and Edward and William Warburton.

Because Astbury neither signed or marked his ware and no records of his production exist, it is difficult to assign a particular piece to him. We do know that he created the Portobello Bowl to celebrate Admiral Vernon's capture of the Spanish stronghold of Porto Bello on the Isthmus of Panama in 1739. Made of red earthenware with white relief decorations of ships, fortifications, and figures, the bowl was as popular in the colonies as it was in England. The chances are that Lawrence Washington was one of the first to buy one of these bowls because he had fought under the admiral at Panama and respected him so much that he called the Virginia estate he left to his half-brother George "Mount Vernon."

While Astbury and his contemporaries fashioned both salt-glazed wares and simply painted figures by hand, latter Staffordshire potters used molds to form a clay cavalcade of nineteenth-century life that marched across English mantelpieces. Their gaily-colored depictions of everyday activities and humorous incidents, portrait busts and statuettes of famous and infamous people, pastille burners in the shape of cottages and castles, and the wide variety of "Toby" jugs (which owe their name to mythical Toby Fillpot, "a thirsty old soul") are folk art at its best.

Although this ware eventually became one of the most important products of the Potteries, most eighteenth-century Staffordshire clay workers made utilitarian items that became more attractive as the use of molds increased. As indicated, molds had been used for some time to impress spriggs and barbotine decorations, but they were unsatisfactory as the clay stuck to them despite constant oiling. About 1730, a new type of mold was developed. It was made from Derbyshire alabaster which was carved into shaped blocks from which porous clay molds were pressed. When one of the

*A Chelsea covered melon tureen and cabbage-leaf plate, 1755.*

"pitchers" wore out it was easily replaced by another cast from the alabaster master pattern. While this process was a great improvement, it was discarded in 1745 when Ralph Daniel—who had introduced the enameling of earthenware and of salt-glazed pottery into Staffordshire—brought from France the secret of plaster of Paris molds.

The new molds were most successfully employed by Thomas Whieldon (1719-1795), last of the Staffordshire peasant potters. Whieldon began potting in his cottage at Fenton Low, fashioning agateware. Whenever he accumulated a large stock, the potter turned salesman and peddled his products. Before long, Whieldon was the owner of a large pottery where he constantly experimented with clays, colors, and glazes, while making every type of Staffordshire ware, including figurines so like John Astbury's that collectors—unable to distinguish the hand that modeled them—call the type Astbury-Whieldon.

Because Whieldon was far more interested in creating novel shapes and in color than in commonplace wares, he made little effort to find customers for the cream-white pottery he developed, although it was superior to that of his competitors. Actually, Whieldon was prouder of his agate, marbled, and tortoiseshell tableware, although he never produced a complete dinner service. Other products of his kilns included gilt-decorated black pottery which resembles the famous Jackfield ware, vessels in the shape of vegetables and fruit whose colors duplicate nature's, and doll's dishes—the first made in Staffordshire for commercial purposes.

Strangely enough, Whieldon never patented his fruit and vegetable ware which was popular on both sides of the Atlantic—the "collyflower" selling very well in America. Nevertheless, he was an astute businessman, as his account books show, and probably realized that a patent would provide no protection since potters went from one pottery to another and shared the knowledge they had gained with each new employer.

Moreover, Staffordshire courts had little respect for patents. Ralph Shaw —the first potter to mix clay in liquid form in a fire-heated container instead of using the sun to evaporate the excess water—found this out in 1736. Shaw, who specialized in sgraffito decoration, had been granted a patent for making white stoneware by a process well known throughout the Potteries and sued John Mitchell of Burslem Hill Top for infringement. The judge, after listening to the charge, handed down a decision that was to send Shaw to France (where he established a pottery), and filled Staffordshire with delight: "Go home, potters, and make whatever kinds of pots you please."

To make pots—and other wares—Whieldon employed a large staff and was the first English potter to hire a full-time modeler with professional training: John Voyez, who was to give Whieldon's future partner Josiah Wedgwood considerable trouble. Among the block-cutters who carved the molds used at Fenton Low was Aaron Wood (1717-1785), a master of his craft who had assisted Astbury in creating the Portobello Bowl. Other members of Aaron's family were equally talented, his brother Ralph (1715-1742) and his nephew Ralph II (1748-1795) being responsible for some of the finest examples of Staffordshire figures and Tobies. Enoch Wood (1759-1840)—Aaron's youngest son—is celebrated not only as a modeler of statuettes (including clay representations of American national heroes designed for the overseas market) but also for making the first collection of Staffordshire pottery.

While the craftsmen who worked in and around the Five Towns were very skilled, the individuals who fashioned porcelain figurines and table-

LEFT: *"St. Paul" by Enoch Wood, Burslem, about 1787.*

RIGHT: *Chelsea figure of soft paste porcelain, "Vauxhall Singer."*

ware were artists. Their creations, imaginatively conceived, beautifully designed and richly colored, are ceramic masterpieces.

As indicated, porcelain was imported into England at an early date and proudly displayed by its wealthy owners. Anxious to cater to this luxury trade, English potters first attempted to reproduce porcelain in 1506. However, because they lacked knowledge of porcelain's components, they were as unsuccessful as Dwight and the others granted patents for making "purslane."

There are two types of porcelain: hard paste and soft paste. The former originated in China during the Tang dynasty (A.D. 618-907). This is true porcelain, consisting of a blend of kaolin (a clay named for the Pass of Kaoling in the Province of Kaoling where it was first found) and the natural silicate of alumina, commonly called petuntse. When fired at a very high temperature, these two natural earths fuse with the overlying glaze into an extremely hard vitreous substance that cannot be scratched with a blade, rings clearly when lightly tapped, and breaks with a smooth fracture which exposes a fine grain of compact texture.

Soft paste porcelain is a combination of various mixtures of clay, sand, and glass to which animal or mineral ingredients have been added. It vitrifies at a comparatively low temperature, varies in hardness—all soft paste porcelains can be easily scratched except those containing soapstone—and feels rough to the touch when broken.

The first true porcelain manufactured in Europe was created in 1709 by Johann Friedrich Boettger, alchemist to the court of Saxony. But British potters, unaware of native deposits of kaolin and petuntse, were unable to duplicate his accomplishment. Meanwhile, Oriental porcelain was being sold by auction at the India Warehouse in Leadenhall Street. The auctioneer would light a candle as each lot was put up, and the bidding lasted until it burned down an inch. "Candle auctions" were well attended and china merchants—china and porcelain are synonymous, the word china being derived from the country of the ware's origin—had no difficulty disposing of their purchases. In fact, England was suffering from "China-mania."

Daniel Defoe, the author of *Robinson Crusoe* and a failure as a tile manufacturer, wrote scathingly about those who piled china to "the tops of ceilings," and Addison's *Spectator*, after reporting that Englishwomen were bartering clothes for china, suggested that they would show more sense to collect "the useful products of our British potteries." However, their writings were ignored. There was good reason. Even the potters realized that their finest wares could not compete with hard paste porcelain imported from the Orient and the Continent.

Therefore, they began making soft paste porcelain, using the formula developed by the French scientist René Antoine Ferchault de Réaumur

(1683-1757). Réaumur's formula—or variations of it—was employed by all English porcelain makers during the eighteenth century with the exception of those in Bristol, New Hall, and Plymouth. In these potteries, hard paste porcelain was produced, following the discovery of native supplies of kaolin and petuntse.

The first English soft paste works was founded at Chelsea by Thomas Briand and Charles Gouyn about 1743. Managed by a former French silversmith, Nicholas Sprimont (1716-1771), Chelsea fashioned well-designed and richly colored porcelain articles. Sprimont modeled many of them, copying in paste the creations of his fellow silversmiths. Besides making "silver shape" ware, Sprimont also developed a formula for soft paste that gave Chelsea modelers a thicker body with which to work, and with it they produced some of the most beautiful of English porcelain—birds, portrait busts, and representations of classical and contemporary subjects. Joseph Willems, who had learned his craft in Belgium, not only modeled many of these articles but also was a painter of the exquisitely designed and delicately colored "Chelsea Toys"—bonbonnières, smelling bottles, snuff boxes, needle cases, miniature seals topped with amatory sentiments (used to impress the wax on love letters), and "Trinkets for Watches . . . in various beautiful Shapes . . . curiously painted in Enamel."

Because soft paste would not hold its shape until fired, Willems and his fellow modelers first fashioned a ware from clay, then made a plaster of Paris mold of it. Actually, several molds were made for figures—head, limbs,

LEFT: *Chelsea soft paste figure of a carpenter, after a Meissen original, 1755.* BELOW: *A plaster block for molding a bowl, Staffordshire, about 1750.*

and body—and assembled by "repairers" who smoothed the seam marks, added the details of dress with wood or metal tools, and used brass dies to form such objects as tree trunks. The later were not only ornamental but also supported the figure during the firing.

At first, the paste was pressed into the mold by hand and, after it had dried and shrunk, removed. If an early figurine is open at the base, this "hand pressing" is revealed by irregularly thick walls and finger marks. Eventually, the sectional molds were fitted together and the paste poured through a hole. When a crust was fixed, the excess paste was poured out, resulting in a smooth, thin-walled figure.

In 1756 Chelsea ceased operations but reopened two years later. However, Sprimont, plagued by ill health and financial difficulties, sold the Chelsea Porcelain Manufactory to James Cox in 1769. Cox, in turn, resold it to William Duesbury (1725-1786), owner of the Derby porcelain works. Before becoming a potter, Duesbury had been an independent enameler of porcelain in London, ornamenting white ware to customers' specifications. In 1754 he became associated with Longton Hall, the first Staffordshire porcelain pottery, which is celebrated for "Snowmen" (white statuettes on unglazed bases), brilliantly painted figures, and molded tableware.

While Sadler and Green ornamented much of the latter with black transfers, most of it was painted by skilled artists including Duesbury, John Hayfield, and a number of unknown craftsmen who have been named by collectors on the basis of their choice of subjects and technique. Thus two of the artists who decorated the "New and Curious Porcelain or China"

BELOW: *Large oval dish from the service made at Chelsea for Warren Hastings, governor-general of India.* RIGHT: *Pair of Bow white busts of Mongolians, 1760.*

made at Longton Hall are referred to as the "Trembly Rose Painter" and the "Castle Painter."

In 1755, Duesbury established his own porcelain works at Derby where soft paste ware had been made since 1749 by André Planché, son of a former Meissen modeler. After serving his apprenticeship to a London jeweler, the young Planché had settled in Derby. As a hobby he experimented in making porcelain and sent his creations to the Cockpit Hill Pot Manufactory to be fired. These pieces attracted the attention of John Heath, one of the owners of Cockpit Hill, who hired Planché to supervise a new department—the Derby Porcelain Manufactory which produced figures in white.

Planché sent much of his output to Duesbury's London shop to be enameled until the latter—after securing financial backing from Heath—opened his Derby Porcelain Company with Planché as manager. Although Planché resigned within a few months, by 1757 Duesbury was so successful that he had enlarged his plant, hired more workmen, and was advertising his porcelain as ". . . the second Dresden."

This boast was typical of Duesbury, who was not a modest man. Actually, his products were inferior until he acquired the porcelain works at Chelsea in 1770, which he kept open until 1783. In that year, models, molds, and all the workers who wished to join him were removed to Derby. Meanwhile, Duesbury utilized fully the colors developed at Chelsea and strengthened his paste by following the Chelsea formula which called for bone ash in the frit (a word used by both glassmakers and potters of soft paste por-

*Pair of Derby figures of musicians in flowered bowers, 1765.*

83

celain to describe the material from which their wares are made).

During the Chelsea-Derby period, Duesbury employed outstanding modelers, including Joseph Hill, Isaac Farnsworth, Pierre Stephan, and John Bacon. The last-named was a famous sculptor, inventor of a machine for roughing out the general shape of a piece of marble to be carved, and winner of the Royal Academy's first gold medal. Duesbury's artists were equally talented: "Jockey" Hill and Zachariah Boreman (who had been chief painter at Chelsea), specialists in landscapes; George Complin, noted for his fruit; and a number of painters who decorated wares with representatives of flowers. This group included Edward Withers, William Corden, and William Billingsley.

Apprenticed to Duesbury in 1774, Billingsley stayed at Derby until 1795 when he was replaced by William Pegg. A painstaking craftsman, Billingsley often built up a rose petal by petal, firing the ware after each painting. His style is so distinctive that collectors easily recognize his work from that of his imitators, for even John Stansby, who had been trained by Billingsley, could not capture his master's mannerisms.

In 1775 Duesbury bought the models and molds of the recently closed porcelain works at Bow near London. Founded by Thomas Fryre—the first potter to use bone ash in a soft paste porcelain frit—Bow is famous for its copies of Oriental wares, imitations of Meissen figures, vases, magnificent china portraits, birds, animals, and elaborate tableware. Among the latter is the misnamed Bow partridge service—the birds are actually Chinese quail.

Duesbury was now the most important porcelain manufacturer in England, having but one major competitor—the porcelain works at Worcester established in 1751 by John Wall, doctor of medicine, portrait painter, and

*No other animal or bird model delights collectors of Bow porcelain more than those of squirrels.*

*Set of three Bloor Derby jardinieres, 1765.*

designer of stained glass. Moreover, Duesbury controlled most of the enameling of porcelain for private customers, having acquired the china shop of John Giles of London who not only employed a large staff of painters but also supplied enamel colors to potters throughout England.

When Duesbury died in 1786 his son William II assumed control of the pottery and added to its staff several distinguished craftsmen, including Richard Askew, who decorated ware with figure subjects, and Jean-Jacques Spanger, perhaps the most famous of Derby modelers. However, the second William was not well and, needing assistance, formed a partnership in 1795 with Michael Kean, a miniaturist. On Duesbury's death the following year, Kean took full charge and, shortly afterward, married his former partner's widow.

Under Kean, Derby produced little of merit. Moreover, his attempt to introduce woman painters led to the resignation of Billingsley and several of his fellow artists. As a result, the quality of Derby porcelain deteriorated and it sold poorly. Therefore, in 1811, Kean was delighted to sell his share of the business to William Sheffield, father-in-law of William Duesbury III. Four years later Sheffield resold the now nearly bankrupt concern to Robert Bloor.

By producing inexpensive articles, cheaply painting the accumulated stock of white ware, and cutting costs wherever possible, Bloor managed not only to keep Derby operating but also to make a profit. However, he became insane in 1845 and, three years later, the pottery was closed.

A number of former Derby craftsmen under the leadership of William Locker then established a small pottery where they made bone china. However, the present-day Royal Crown Derby Porcelain Company—one of England's most successful potteries—was not founded until 1876 and has no connection with the original works.

Meanwhile, at Worcester, the only major English porcelain manufactory launched in the eighteenth century that has continued uninterrupted production to modern times was thriving. Its soft paste was harder than that made elsewhere and, as it contained soapstone, could withstand boiling water—which other soft pastes could not do. Moreover, the glaze used at Worcester was heat-resistant and rarely crazed as did that of most English porcelains.

When Dr. John Wall and his associates established Worcester they planned to produce only well-designed and decorated, inexpensive porcelain domestic wares. However, they soon discovered that it was a costly process to hand paint the underglaze blue ornamentation of their imitations of Chinese imports. Therefore, Robert Hancock, who had done much of the engraving for Janssen's Battersea enamel works, had little difficulty in persuading Dr. Wall to employ transfer printing to ornament his wares.

A master of the art of copperplate engraving, Hancock supplied Wall with both original compositions and reproductions of famous paintings. Perhaps the most famous of his own work is the portrait of Frederick the Great of Prussia that appeared on mugs made in 1757. Hancock signed this plate with his rebus of a gamecock perched upon a hand. Another Worcester engraver, Richard Holdship, also used a rebus—an anchor.

Strangely enough, after adopting transfer printing, Wall began producing luxury wares. Between 1764 and 1783, Worcester's kilns fired well-modeled porcelain tableware decorated in rich colors. Its designs were painted by talented artists—many formerly employed at Chelsea—who imitated the work of Continental ceramic craftsmen. They were also inspired by the traditional ornamentation of Japanese porcelain and created

LEFT: *Worcester yellow-ground dish of the Dr. Wall period.* RIGHT: *Worcester vase with gold foliage against a cream-colored ground.*

*Pieces from a Worcester blue scale tea service, the teapot 6 inches high, 1765.*

a ware known today as Worcester-Japan.

However, there was nothing imitative in the work of those who covered Worcester porcelain with "gorgeous ornithological fantasies." While the subject of the anonymous artist known only as the "Owl Painter" is easily recognized, the rest of Worcester's "rainbow-plumed fowl" resemble nothing in nature.

Far more pedestrian are the decorations of John Donaldson and Jeffreyes Hammett O'Neale, who was responsible for one of Chelsea's best-selling wares—a tea service bearing scenes from Aesop's Fables. Both Donaldson and O'Neale painted vases and jars, the former specializing in rural subjects, the latter in hunting scenes and landscapes. In addition to being ornamented by staff artists, Worcester porcelain was also painted by free-lance enamelers, including John Giles.

From 1772 on, the Worcester works underwent a series of managerial changes. In 1840 it was completely reorganized and merged with another Worcester porcelain manufactory operated by Thomas Grainger. Then, in 1862, the company assumed the name under which it is now known—the Worcester Royal Porcelain Company.

While Bow, Chelsea, Derby, and Worcester were the most important soft paste porcelain works, smaller porcelain potteries—Caughley, Liverpool, Lowestoft, Madeley, Nantgarw, New Hall, and Swansea produced excellent wares. Moreover, it was at Bristol—site of the fourth soft paste

*The owners of the Lowestoft pottery on the Suffolk coast—where this soft paste, braided-handled cruet and cup and saucer were made—operated only one kiln because they were actively engaged in the herring industry.*

pottery to be established in England—that William Cookworthy (1705-1780) made true porcelain after discovering kaolin and petuntse in Cornwall. Unable to secure the services of trained workmen in his native Plymouth, Cookworthy removed his plant to Bristol in 1770 where he made "Desert Services, ornamental figures, Candlesticks, and many other valuable articles."

Until 1773—the year in which Cookworthy sold his works to Richard Champion, a fellow Quaker who operated a Bristol pottery—only run-of-the-kiln wares were produced. Most were copies of popular silver patterns, Oriental imports, and poorly decorated tableware. Moreover, Cookworthy's figures—many of which were made in molds acquired from other potteries—were poorly modeled and painted.

Under Champion, quality improved. He fashioned well-shaped tableware, including presentation services, decorated in polychrome colors. One such set was made to commemorate the election of Edmund Burke to Parliament as a Member for Bristol, Champion being a close friend of the great English statesman. Champion's craftsmen also fashioned portrait plaques and vases ornamented with carefully modeled figures in high relief. Certain of these pieces were painted by the same artists who ornamented Bristol's famous blue glass, but much was decorated by artists trained on the Continent.

Bristol porcelain sold well and Champion was convinced that he would accumulate a fortune. However, he was a cautious businessman and left nothing to chance. Therefore, seven years before the expiration date of Cookworthy's patent—which he controlled—he applied for a fourteen-year extension of the privilege of having the exclusive right to manufacture hard paste porcelain from English materials. Because a group of Staffordshire potters contested his plea, a long and bitter legal fight ensued. Eventually, Champion won the suit but the expense had been tremendous.

Fortunately, this placed no burden on Champion. Not only was he operating a successful pottery but also he was the owner of a fleet of merchantmen trading with the American colonies. But three months after receiving the extension on his patent, a law was passed forbidding English merchants to ship goods to the rebellious Americans. As Champion had been shipping much of his output overseas, this embargo cut production at Bristol considerably.

Loans from friends enabled Champion to stay in business until the capture of his vessels by the French in 1777, when he was forced to close the pottery. In 1781 he assigned his formula to a group of Staffordshire potters who formed a company to make porcelain at New Hall. It was understood that Champion would act as manager of the works, but shortly after the company was organized he withdrew from the venture. His old friend Edmund Burke had secured for him the post of Deputy Paymaster-General to the Forces, a position he held until the Tories came into power in 1784. Unemployed, Champion then migrated to South Carolina where he died.

Meanwhile, despite the demand for porcelain, the kilns of the Potteries were filling the air with clouds of dense black smoke. No individual was more responsible for this than Josiah Wedgwood (1730-1795), the most celebrated of English potters.

*Part of a 45-piece Swansea dessert service, once the property of the Marquis of Exeter.*

The son, grandson, great-grandson, brother, cousin, and nephew of potters, Wedgwood was apprenticed in 1744 to his elder brother Thomas who fired kilns at Burslem. Upon completing his indenture, Josiah asked for a partnership and, when refused, secured financial backing from John Harrison, a tradesman, and opened his own pottery. However, their arrangement proved unsatisfactory and Wedgwood formed a partnership with Whieldon that lasted for five years. It was an ideal collaboration—Whieldon was a practical potter with great technical skill, while Wedgwood had a bent for experimenting with new wares.

Because white salt-glazed stoneware was costly to make—being brittle it broke easily during firing—and since it had been replaced by porcelain on many English tables, Wedgwood spent much of his time developing a cheap but attractive earthenware. Mixing calcined flint and various clays, he finally produced a cream-colored ware that had "all the advantages of being fashionable, and looking expensive, combined with ease of manufacture, durability and comparative cheapness."

Despite constant pain in his right knee—the result of a childhood infection—which was increased by an injury that eventually made amputation necessary, Wedgwood continued to improve his "cream color," seek new glazes, and experiment. He was even more active after 1795 when his partnership with Whieldon ended. After hiring the Ivy House Pottery at Burslem from two of his uncles, Wedgwood formed another partnership for the making of "useful" wares with his cousin Thomas Wedgwood. Limited in capital, Josiah made molds, mixed clay, supervised firing, tended to the books, and contacted customers. He also improved technical processes and taught his employees to use the turning-lathe to create ornamental effects.

In 1762 Wedgwood hired a larger pottery, the Brick House Works in Burslem. It was here that he made a breakfast set of cream-colored ware for presentation to Queen Charlotte of England. Her Majesty, delighted

FAR LEFT: *"Strawberry" cup and saucer—one of the most sought after Staffordshire patterns.*

LEFT: *Pineapple ware, Whieldon-type teapot, 1750-1770.*

ABOVE: *Hand-enameled soup tureen in cream-colored Queen's ware.*

RIGHT: *Wedgwood and Bentley black basalt two handled vase and cover, 1774.*

with the gift, immediately ordered a complete dinner service of the same material and appointed Wedgwood Queen's Potter. A clever businessman, Wedgwood named his product Queen's Ware—and this label plus the quality of "cream color" assured his success.

Originally, Queen's Ware was decorated by Ann Warburton, widow of John Warburton, the celebrated Staffordshire enameler and the mother of Jacob Warburton, one of the group that acquired Champion's patent. Later, Wedgwood sent the ware to Sadler and Green to be ornamented by transfer printing, often accompanying his shipments to Liverpool. It was during one of these trips that he met Thomas Bentley, the merchant who became his partner in 1768.

Meanwhile, Wedgwood had married his distant cousin Sarah Wedgwood, opened his first London showroom under the direction of his brother John, and acquired a large estate in Shelton. Here he built Etruria, a village comprising shops, kilns, storehouses, his own home, and comfortable housing for his employees. In an age when employers had little interest in the welfare of their workers, Wedgwood provided his staff with excellent working conditions. However, he insisted on high standards of workmanship and was apt to stride through the pottery, cane in hand, smashing pieces that did not meet with his approval.

Until 1773 when the "useful" works at Burslem were removed to Shelton, only ornamental wares were made at Etruria. Wedgwood had a great interest in decorative pieces and spent much of his time trying to improve his new black-stained, finely grained, very hard stoneware which he had named basaltes because of its resemblance to an Egyptian marble of that name. Upon succeeding, he carefully recorded the results of his experiments in a cypher of his own invention, then turned his attention to something else. Torn between the creative impulse of the artist and the practical attitude of the businessman, Wedgwood frankly admitted, "The greatest difficulty I ever found was to check and keep my inventions under proper subordination."

Busy as he was at the pottery, Wedgwood found time to play an im-

*Two collector's items of Staffordshire origin. The pitcher on the left is copper lustre, the one on the right silver resist.*

*Queen's ware plates, including two trial specimens from the famous service made for Catherine the Great.*

portant part in securing better roads for Staffordshire and in the building of the Grand Trunk Canal. He was also active in the abolitionist movement and other liberal causes. Nevertheless, he never neglected potting. From his constant experimentation came many new pastes and bodies: rosso-antico, an improvement on the common red ware of the Potteries; cane-colored ware painted with enamels or ornamented with reliefs; lustre, made by coating clay with metallic oxides of gold or platinum; pearl, an extremely white body; and jasper ware.

The latter is the best known of all his creations—powder blue jasper ornamented with raised white figures being the one Wedgwood ware most people recognize. Before perfecting jasper, the master potter of Etruria concocted ten thousand different formulas and expended a fortune. But Wedgwood never counted time or costs when experimenting.

Besides creating new bodies, Wedgwood also fashioned original forms, his pattern books listing forty teapots of various shapes and nearly three hundred types of vases. In addition to "useful" wares he potted many luxury items: cameos, intaglios, subject medallions, plaques, tablets, lamps, candleholders, figurines, and a great number of small pieces ranging in size from door knobs to toothpicks. These items are known as "Applied Wedgwood," being combined with crystal, bronze, silver, and steel by master metal workers.

The skill of these craftsmen was no greater than that of those who modeled and decorated Wedgwood's wares. Some of the finest artists of the day worked for Wedgwood—George Stubbs, the most outstanding horse painter in the history of European art; James Tassie, a famous engraver of gems: and John Flaxman, the eminent sculptor. Wedgwood also employed talented amateurs (including several women painters) and kept a large staff of Italian artists busy in Rome copying ancient works of art under the direction of Henry Webber.

However, despite the talents of his craftsmen, Wedgwood constantly altered their work and, convinced that the firm's mark on a piece was more important than the signature of its maker, allowed few pieces to be signed. This ruling makes identification of the work of a particular artist most difficult.

Creative himself, Wedgwood had a pleasant relationship with his artists. The only exception was John Voyez, carver of seals and moldmaker, whose improper conduct resulted in his imprisonment. Fearful that on his release Voyez would carry Etruria's secrets to another pottery, Wedgwood offered to pay him a salary on condition he would not accept any employment. Typically, Voyez agreed—and immediately went to work for a rival firm.

Many of the special orders Wedgwood received brought more prestige

LEFT: *Wedgwood vase with cover, sometimes known as the "Pegasus Vase."* RIGHT: *Superb Wedgwood slate blue Portland vase, 9½ inches high, about 1790.*

to Etruria's craftsmen than profit to the firm. But none ever cost Wedgwood money. For example, the fee paid for the Russian Imperial Service—popularly called the "Frog Service" as it was designed for the use of Catherine the Great at the Palace of *La Grenouillers* (frog marsh)—barely met the cost of making it. However, before shipping the 950-piece service to Russia, Wedgwood exhibited part of it in his London showroom. Visitors admired the samples of the 1,282 views of Great Britain that ornamented the service and chuckled at the green frogs Nathaniel Cooper had painted on it instead of the coat-of-arms that traditionally were placed on imperial services—and, far more important to Wedgwood, many of the sight-seers, anxious to have tableware made by a potter to royalty, made purchases.

Meanwhile Wedgwood continued his experiments and improved potting techniques. In 1883 he invented the pyrometre, an instrument that made the accurate measurement of oven heat possible for the first time. As a result, he was elected a Fellow of the Royal Society but had little time to attend meetings because Bentley's death in 1780 had increased his responsibilities. Finally, in 1790, he admitted that he needed assistance and took his three sons and nephew into partnership. That same year, after four years of work, Wedgwood succeeded in reproducing the famous Portland Vase in jasper. In 1858, when a lunatic smashed this priceless relic—then on exhibit in the British Museum—experts were able to reconstruct it by using one of Wedgwood's jasper copies as a model.

Plagued by ill health, Wedgwood gradually withdrew from active management of the firm. On January 3, 1795, death came to Josiah Wedgwood, "the only potter of whom it may be truly said that the whole course of pottery manufacture had been influenced by his individuality, skill, and taste."

During Wedgwood's lifetime he had both rivals and copyists. None of the latter annoyed him more than Humphrey Palmer of Hanley who boldly reproduced his creations—securing models by sending his wife in disguise to Wedgwood's London showrooms to buy new patterns as they were placed on sale. Actually, Wedgwood could do nothing about Palmer—or the others who stole his ideas—for he held no patents except one for his method of encaustic painting (the ornamentation of black ware with red decorations in imitation of the embellishments on vases found in Etruscan sites). However, Palmer, who had developed a similar technique, forced Wedgwood to share the patent rights. But nothing the "unscrupulous pirate" did irked Wedgwood more than the hiring of Voyez after the latter left Etruria in disgrace.

Wedgwood's relationship with Palmer was an exception because Wedgwood was very friendly with his neighbors and competitors, many of whom had learned their craft at Etruria or were related to him by blood

LEFT: *Earthenware jug, Ralph Wood the Younger, modeled by John Voyez.* RIGHT: *Salopian pitcher made at Caughley from clay taken from the same beds used by Roman potters during the occupation of England.*

or marriage. Thus he often turned to his rivals for help when his kilns could not produce enough "useful" ware to meet an order or for such specialties as the lead-glaze figurines made by the Ralph Woods, father and son.

Actually, some of Wedgwood's closest friends were his keenest competitors: William Adams, a former apprentice and "one clever pupil" whose basalt and jasper pieces can be distinguished from those of his master only by their marks; Jacob Warburton, who took time out from selling his pottery on the Continent to represent Wedgwood during his legal battle with Palmer; and John Turner, maker of "cream color" and other useful wares from the Cornwall clay mined in pits leased jointly with Wedgwood. Turner was not only a master potter—he once fashioned a complete ceramic banquet from stoneware—but also a constant experimenter like Wedgwood. His sons John and William were also clever craftsmen, the former becoming manager of the pottery Thomas Minton (1765-1836) established at Stoke.

Minton had learned the art of engraving as an apprentice to Thomas Turner, owner of the Caughley pottery and an outstanding colorist. Turner invented the distinctive blue with which the famous Willow Pattern—first made at Caughley—was printed from a copper plate engraved by Minton. Traditionally, this ware depicts an Oriental tale—two lovers fleeing across a willow-shaded bridge pursued by the girl's father. But legend is more romantic than truth. The design is merely an adaptation of one Turner saw in France while learning to make porcelain. In 1798 Turner sold the Caughley works and his formulas to a former apprentice, John Rose, and, fifteen years later, Rose removed the plant to his pottery in Coalport on the other side of the Severn River.

At Coalport Rose experimented with bone china, made excellent porcelain and "useful" wares, and perfected a lustrous white glaze which earned him a gold medal and the eternal gratitude of potters because it eliminated their greatest occupational hazard—paralysis caused by the presence of lead and arsenic in other glazes. Finally, the Coalport organization was acquired in 1925 by the Cauldron Potteries which had been established in 1780 by Job Ridgeway, who had served his apprenticeship under Wedgwood.

In 1768 Thomas Whieldon noted in his accounts: "Hired Siah Spode to give him from this time to Martelmas 2/3 or 2/6 if he deserves it."

Josiah Spode (1733-1797) soon proved that he was worthy of the higher weekly wage. Five years later he was earning seven shillings, six pence as a journeyman potter. In 1770 Spode went into business for himself at Stoke-upon-Trent and produced jugs and other utilitarian wares. Aided by Thomas Lucas, an engraver, and James Richards, a printer, both formerly at Caughley, Spode experimented in improving Turner's method of decorating white earthenware by blue transfer printing. The technical processes he eventually developed are still used to ornament inexpensive wares. Spode's blue-underglaze-printed tablewares sold well and, as a result, he opened a London warehouse under the direction of his son Josiah II and William Copeland.

Because his London office attended to all business transactions, Spode was free to formulate new bodies and glazes, design molds, and to experiment with kaolin and petuntse. Out of his investigations came bone china —a combination of the components of hard paste porcelain and calcined ox bones—which not only was less costly to make than true porcelain but also had a translucent body that lent itself to underglaze decoration. The new ware became very popular—today, bone china is the leading export ware of England—and was imitated by other potters.

When Spode died, Josiah II made Copeland his partner and devoted himself to improving his father's formula for bone china, developing new decorations (although former Oriental designs were not discarded), and creating porcelain dinner services ornamented with colorful birds. Young Spode also made stoneware, having acquired John Turner's formula, despite the fact that his hard earthenware competed with Mason's Patent Ironstone China, the invention of Charles James Mason, husband of Sarah Spode.

Copeland died in 1826, Josiah II the following year, and the management

97

The pottery at Leeds in Yorkshire produced much ware similar to that made in Staffordshire. This horse was modeled about 1795.

ABOVE: *An exquisite pink-and-white Minton bone china egg server and cups.*

LEFT: *This Staffordshire figure of Jenny Lind in Donizetti's La Figlia del Reggimento was made in 1860.*

of the works was assumed by Josiah III until his death in 1833. Control of the firm then passed to William Taylor Copeland and William Garrett. For some time the names of these men were impressed upon wares, then only Copeland's name was used with the addition *Late Spode* until 1867 when the mark was changed to Copeland alone. The present-day factory uses various marks that combine the names of Spode and Copeland.

By the middle of the nineteenth century, mechanization had replaced most hand operations in English potteries. Although craftsmen appreciated engine-turned wheels and lathes, they feared new techniques would eliminate the need for skilled artisans. However, few reacted so violently to the introduction of machinery as did John Doe of Bristol. Doe, a leading underglaze-blue painter, killed himself when his employer shifted to transfer printing.

Actually, the Great Exhibition of 1851 showed that machinery was debasing English potting. Nevertheless, skilled artists were in demand. The craftsmen who fashioned many of the Parian (unglazed porcelain imitative of Parian marble) figures that graced Victorian parlors were worthy successors to the Woods; while Thomas Minton, who had greatly expanded the pottery founded by his father, employed Walter Crane, famous as an illustrator of children's books; Carrier-Belluse, the sculptor who taught Rodin; and Louis Solon, one of the greatest of all potters. Among Solon's many achievements is the invention of the pâte-sur-pâte decorative process which is best described as "a cloud of cream in a cup of tea."

The skill of this trio and of their fellow craftsmen who worked in various English potteries during the nineteenth century is matched by the artist-potters who now mold and ornament wares in the sprawling modern plants operated by Derby, Doulton, Minton, Spode, Wedgwood, and Worcester. Although primarily concerned with mass production, all these firms depend upon the creative genius of their designers and decorators to fashion both "useful" wares and ornamental pieces.

Nor has the free-lance potter vanished from the countryside. Bernard Leach, Staite Murray, Michael Cardew, Norah Braden, and Tibor Reich— to name but a few—still carry on the proud traditions of an ancient craft.

# 4

## Silver

When Alfred fled the Danes across the marshes to the Isle of Athelney in A.D. 878, he dropped a gold brooch bearing the inscription AEFRED MEC HEWT GEW(E)RCAN—"Alfred had me made." While authorities differ as to whether the enameled portrait on the Alfred Jewel—which was unearthed by a plow and is now displayed at Oxford's Ashmolean Museum—is that of the king or another, they are agreed that the brooch Alfred dropped is of English origin.

There is good reason for this attribution, because artisans were working precious metals in England at a very early date. Their work was highly regarded throughout Europe and, during the eighth and ninth centuries, a large number of English goldsmiths—until recently "goldsmith" meant a worker in either gold or silver—had their own quarter in Rome near the Vatican where they made wares for church use. These craftsmen not only employed the techniques that had been developed in their native land but also the methods they had learned from the Continental metalworkers Alfred invited to his court.

However, the most outstanding English silversmiths of the Anglo-Saxon era were members of religious orders who had obeyed King Edgar's decree that "every priest, to increase knowledge, diligently learn some handicraft." As the Dark Ages cast a pall over Europe, lay brothers, monks, and abbots working in the shadows of cathedrals and monasteries kept the art of silversmithing alive, fashioning, among other wares, richly ornamented ecclesiastical vessels, statues of saints overlaid with precious stones, and covers for the Gospel decorated with religious scenes. The latter were modeled in relief by repoussé—the working with hammer and punches on the back of the metal which was fixed in a yielding material.

While the smiths at Canterbury, Ely, Evesham, and St. Albans produced creations "which surpassed the material," the most famous of all ecclesiastical silversmiths was Saint Dunstan of Glastonbury who, at the age of twenty-four, became Archbishop of Canterbury. Dunstan, born in 925,

*Ecclesiastical silver of the Anglo-Saxon period is very rare. This Queen Anne plain censer and incense boat were made much later, in 1708, by Benjamin Pyne.*

learned his craft as a simple monk and practiced it at Glastonbury Abbey. According to tradition, the Devil materialized over his forge one day, whereupon the quick-witted monk seized the fiend by the nose with red-hot tongs, releasing him only after receiving a promise that he would never bother Dunstan again. The Wardens and Commonalty of the Mystery of Goldsmiths of the City of London paid tribute to Dunstan when they received the first of their many charters in 1327 (members of the craft had banded informally as early as 1180), choosing him as the craft's patron saint.

Both ecclesiastical and secular silver of the Anglo-Saxon period is very rare. Most of it, including the treasures William the Conqueror removed from abbeys and cathedrals and distributed to French churches, eventually met the fate of almost all early silver—being thrown into the melting pot either to be reworked into new plate to meet the demands of changing fashion or to provide bullion to pay the costs of war.

The expansion of trade during the latter centuries of the Middle Ages brought prosperity to English silversmiths: from royalty came commissions for plate; wealthy merchants ordered silver basins, chargers, cups, salts, and spoons for their tables; patrons of education presented colleges with elaborate pieces; and the devout bought ecclesiastical vessels to give to churches.

As the demand for wrought silver increased, the list of regulations governing its manufacture lengthened. Certain of these rules were established by the craftsmen themselves: others were imposed by the King and Parliament. However, there was little opposition to these laws from silversmiths since the majority of them confirmed the privileges of their guild.

Therefore, when Henry II ordered the Mayor and Aldermen of London to appoint "six discreet goldsmiths of the City" to oversee their craft, silversmiths were delighted because the royal command made possible the closing of shops operated by unregistered, poorly trained, or dishonest smiths.

Actually, it was very easy for a silversmith to cheat his clients. Because pure silver is too soft for practical use, artisans have always mixed it with other metals to harden it—copper proving the most satisfactory alloy since a small amount not only stiffens silver but also makes it easier to work. But an unethical smith could increase the ratio of copper to silver with little fear of detection.

This practice was made illegal in 1300 when Edward I decreed that wrought silver should maintain the same standard as that of his realm's coinage. This was the sterling standard—established by the Easterlings, silversmiths of Central Europe who had refined the royal bullion—consisting of 925 parts pure silver to 1000 parts of metal. Edward ordered the Wardens of the Goldsmiths' Company to enforce his ordinance, instructing them to go "from shop to shop amongst the workers, assaying . . . (and) if they find any worse than the touch, that piece shall be forfeit to the King."

His Majesty also specified that all assayed silver should bear "La tête de leopart"—a punch that has undergone many changes before assuming its present-day form of an uncrowned leopard. Similarly, the lion passant first placed on silver in 1544 when Henry VIII debased the coinage has had a variety of forms. This device was not required by law but was adopted by

*Note the hallmarks, near the handle of the cup and on the base of the candlestick.*

*A 16th-century stoneware jug with silver-gilt mounts.*

the smiths to show that craftsmen maintained the sterling standard even if royalty did not.

From 1363 on, master silversmiths were required to have marks of their own, "known to those who shall be assigned by the King to supervise their works." At first, these hallmarks were symbols, replicas of shop signs, or a rebus representing a smith's name. However, by the end of the seventeenth century it was the practice to use initials as the maker's punch, craftsmen recording the hallmarks they used beside their names in a register kept at the assay office in Goldsmiths' Hall.

While silversmiths had nothing to do with the various marks that showed they had paid the duty levied on their products, in 1478 they originated a date-letter system to identify the year in which a ware was assayed. Although most silver collectors find it necessary to consult books listing the various date-letters to determine when a piece was made, the system itself is not complicated. For example, by disregarding J, V, W, X, Y, and Z, London craftsmen could use the other letters of the alphabet for a cycle of twenty years—the type of letter and the appearance of its enclosing shield being changed at the beginning of each cycle.

Thus, the hallmarks on silver provide positive proof that its metal is of sterling standard; tell when and where it was made; and, in many cases, make it possible to identify its maker. Moreover, whether self-imposed or established by law, regulations have, for more than six hundred years, assured purchasers of British silver that it is of the highest standard of material and workmanship. Jealous of their reputations as honest craftsmen and proud of their traditions, English silversmiths with very few exceptions have faithfully adhered to both voluntary and mandatory rules, whether fashioning "6 sponez of welke shelles . . . garnished slightle wt silver" in the Middle Ages or a modern ashtray. As a result, England has produced more fine silver than any other nation and her silversmiths have few peers.

The silver wrought by English smiths of the Middle Ages which has survived shows that the smiths understood both the possibilities and limitations of the metal with which they worked. Perhaps the most famous piece created during this period is the Coronation Spoon, used to annoint kings and queens when they assume the English throne. Made of silver-gilt—silver to which a thin layer of gold has been applied—set with four pearls in the broadest part of the handle, its thin bowl divided by a ridge down the center, this relic is the oldest known existing spoon of English manufacture.

During the Middle Ages the only spoons in the huts of serfs were chips of wood or horn, and it is from the Anglo-Saxon *spon* (chip) that the word spoon is derived. However, the spoons of feudal lords were fashioned from silver, while those of royalty were made of gold.

Besides making spoons and cups for those who could afford them, medieval silversmiths also supplied plate to the wealthy. Plate served a double purpose: not only did it do service as a household decoration but also provided its owner with a ready source of cash. Thus, when Edward III traveled to the Continent in 1337, he borrowed plate from nine abbeys with the understanding that, if necessary, he could consign it to the melting pot.

Edward probably had no intention of replacing any plate he reduced to bullion. Otherwise, he would have taken a loan from Sir John de Chichester, the silversmith who made his wedding jewelry, for Sir John, like other members of the craft, engaged in moneylending until the Bank of England was established in 1694. This profitable sideline enabled Sir William Faryngdon to purchase an entire London ward in 1279 which he retained by the token payment of a single "gilliflower" (clove pink) every Easter.

Certain titled silversmiths such as Sir John de Chichester, Sir Martin Bowes, and Sir Hugh Middleton (creator of London's water system and smith to Sir Walter Raleigh) confined their loans to royalty. Others, including Sir Robert Vinter who fashioned Charles II's coronation regalia, not only lent money to those of high rank—Vinter cleared a profit of £ 10,000 on a single loan made to Charles—but also served less noble clients as bankers. "Thence," notes Samuel Pepys in his diary, "to Sir Robert Vinter's leaving clear in his hands £ 2000 of my owne money, to call for when I please."

As the Middle Ages gave way to the Renaissance the craft of silversmithing prospered. To be sure, only churches, colleges, guilds, and the very rich could accumulate large collections of plate, but by the fifteenth century people of moderate means could afford one or two pieces of silver. The increased use of silver is reflected by wills of this period that list bequests of "My best cuppe" or "halfe a dossen sylver spounys with mayden heedes on the end."

"Mayden heedes" are small spoons with narrow, pear-shaped bowls, the

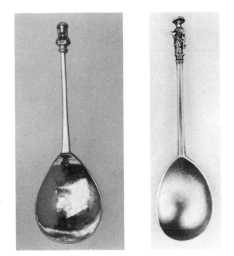

LEFT: *A maidenhead-type spoon, probably late 15th century.* RIGHT: *Made in 1552, this apostle spoon depicts St. Peter.*

handles of which are topped with the head and bust of the Virgin Mary. Among the rarest of English spoons, maidenheads are easily dated because the Virgin's drapery and hair style duplicate the fashion of the day. Incidentally, no article of flat silver has changed more in form and decoration than spoons, and their evolution is one of the most fascinating chapters in the history of silversmithing.

Certain silversmiths specialized in the making of spoons. Among the most outstanding were C. Easton, John Ions, Richard Osborn, and John Lavers, all of Exeter; James Carlisle of Hull; Richard Orenge of Sherborne; Nathaniel Bullen of Chester; and Peter Peterson of Norwich. Peterson, who is credited with making the first cylindrical salt in 1567, was one of the finest smiths of the Tudor Period, working at his bench until his death at the age of eighty-four.

No English silver spoons delight collectors more than "spones with appostells." Introduced from the Continent about 1450—the earliest known spoons of English make topped with silver-gilt figures of the apostles are dated 1478—"postle spones" were favorite christening gifts. However, only wealthy godparents could afford a complete set consisting of the twelve apostles and the Master. The less affluent had to be content with giving only the four Evangelists or but a single spoon depicting the saint for which the infant was named.

Besides fashioning spoons, fifteenth-century smiths made dishes, chargers —the ancestors of modern platters—used to carry meat from spit to table, "cuppes," "basyns," "gobellets," mazers with silver prints set in their bottoms representing secular or sacred devices, and other drinking vessels.

Enameled or gilt prints were also used to decorate the bowls of cups or were inserted into the finials of their covers. Gilding had a practical as well as a decorative value because it prevented tarnishing, being particularly effective in resisting the corrosive action of salt. Therefore, most smiths gilded standing salts, which were made in a wide variety of shapes. But no matter what its form, the standing salt served to indicate the position of those who sat at the high table—the nearer one was to it, the higher his rank.

Because the great landholders melted down their plate in order to pay their soldiers, few examples of the salts, ewers, basins, and other silver owned by the barons before the Wars of the Roses have survived. However, the battle for the English throne did not eliminate the desire to acquire silver, and Henry Tudor, head of the victorious House of Lancaster, accumulated a tremendous collection of plate during his reign as Henry VII. Most of it was simple in form and its ornamentation was inspired by patterns developed during the Gothic Period when "English silver design was at its most English."

No English kings had a greater appreciation of the beauty of wrought silver than the Tudors and none acquired it more cheaply because of "benevolences"—a legal form of theft instituted by Henry VIII. City records and guild ledgers list great numbers of silver articles "Lentt to the King" but there are few notations indicating that these were ever returned.

Much of the plate Henry "borrowed" reflects the impact of the Renaissance on English silversmiths. After resisting the new style, they had gradually turned from graceful shapes and simple ornamentation to elegant forms elaborately decorated with piercing, floral festoons, classical figures, scrolls, masks, and chased scrollwork. Actually, Henry was responsible for this evolution because, in 1526, he invited Hans Holbein, the German painter, to join his Court. Holbein not only painted his royal patron but also did designing for London's leading silversmiths, jewelers, and bookbinders. In following his patterns, metal workers duplicated the rich Renaissance style then popular in Italy and it became so fashionable that much old plate was reworked.

Holbein was not the only German to change English taste in silver. A number of his countrymen plied their craft in London; merchants imported the creations of Bernard Zahn and Hans Brosamer while native artisans frequently consulted Brosamer's *Ein Neu Kuntbuchlein* and other pattern books of German smiths.

As English silversmiths adopted and adapted the designs of Continental craftsmen and decorated their creations with over-all chasing, embossed strapwork, swags of fruit, medallions, scrolls, sea creatures, human and animal figures, the plate listed in Henry's *Jewel Book* became more and more opulent. However, it was often badly proportioned. Nevertheless, it was of sterling standard and, when Henry debased the currency, Englishmen

ABOVE: *These salts were made in the early 18th century.* RIGHT: *Elizabethan gilded silver ostrich egg cup. Smiths were also commissioned to make silver mounts for imported porcelains and coconuts.*

wisely bought plate instead of filling their money chests with the substandard coins the king had struck from the silverware he removed from abbeys and monasteries after establishing the Church of England.

By the time Elizabeth I assumed the throne, this "investment" plate was ornamented with the exotic decorations demanded by Tudor taste. None of it was more elaborate than the "sundry pacelles of gold and silver plate" presented to Elizabeth as gifts on New Year's Day or during a "progress" by subjects seeking her favor.

The tremendous amount of silver shipped to Europe from New World mines during Elizabeth's reign enabled smiths to reduce their prices. As a result, John Eydes and C. Easton of Exeter—along with other craftsmen—found a ready market among the upper middle classes for their silver-mounted Rhenish stoneware. In time, this group became as important a source of income to Elizabethan silversmiths as the wealthy who commissioned useful and ornamental plate or rock crystal and Oriental porcelains in silver mounts.

Despite the fact that leaders of fashion were turning from silver to the glass vessels imported from Venice or made by Verzelini in London, the reduction in the cost of plate increased the use of silver in English homes. Flooded with orders, owners of large shops divided the various steps in fashioning a ware among the members of their staffs. Leaders of the craft bewailed this practice, maintaining that "every perfect workman ought to be skilful in all and be able to begin and end his own work himself as in times past."

Left: *Elizabeth I beaker, 1586.* Center: *Mid-17th-century beaker engraved with foliage in strapwork panels.* Right: *James I silvergilt steeplecup and cover, 1604, maker's mark a bunch of grapes.*

But the fear that silversmiths were losing their skill was ill-founded. English artisans proved they were masters of their craft as they replaced highly decorated church plate with the austere Communion cups of Protestantism and met the demand for plainer domestic silver that marked the last years of Good Queen Bess' rule. They also displayed great talents during the period of prosperity that followed the union of Scotland and England by James I after Elizabeth's death. Encouraged by their extravagant monarch—who had brought George Heriot, an Edinburgh silversmith, with him to London—members of the craft had all the work they could handle. Not only were there commissions from private patrons but also from James who wished to replace the large amount of plate he had turned over to Spain following the signing of a peace treaty.

Although they did not accomplish this task, Jacobean silversmiths did develop a style that was to influence English domestic silver down to the present day. But as the first quarter of the seventeenth century ended, changing economic conditions made it more profitable for silversmiths to lend their silver bars than to work them into plate. Moreover, James' son Charles I was bankrupt and only the most daring commissioned a craftsman because the Crown was seizing private plate and melting it into coins. Because Charles was as willing to replenish his coffers with silver wrought in earlier times as with contemporary creations, many a treasured heirloom was "given" to the Mint by those who wished to avoid imprisonment.

While most of this donated silver was melted down, luxury-loving Charles retained the most ornate examples for his own use. Strangely enough, even as he was destroying irreplaceable relics of the past, Charles encouraged the art of silversmithing when he invited Christiaan van Vianen to join his Court. Van Vianen, the most famous artisan in a family of Dutch silversmiths which dictated the design of wrought silver in Holland for nearly a century, was a master in sculpturing silver in high relief. Native smiths commissioned by members of Charles' own circle—who did not fear confiscation of their plate—tried vainly to duplicate his technique. However, they were most successful in reproducing the extravagant designs of Dutch pattern books.

Meanwhile, despite Charles' grasping hands, members of the middle class were ordering simply ornamented silver from William Maundy, his brother Thomas, and other London craftsmen. A few smiths even received orders for forks, introduced into England by travelers who had brought them back from Italy where they were in common use. But while the first fork known to be made by a British craftsman is dated 1632, the custom of transporting food from plate to mouth with the left hand was not discarded until one hundred years later.

At first thought it would appear unlikely that any early Stuart silver exists. Much of it was thrown into the melting pot to pay the costs of England's Civil War or reduced to a molten mass when the Great Fire swept over London. Moreover, a large amount of the plate which escaped the depredations of cavaliers, Puritans, and the holocaust of 1666 was re-

LEFT: *Charles I slip top spoons dated 1638. Each slip top is engraved with a small cross in a heart.* CENTER: *A 17th-century Puritan spoon.* RIGHT: *William and Mary trefid spoon marked with the date-letter for 1691.*

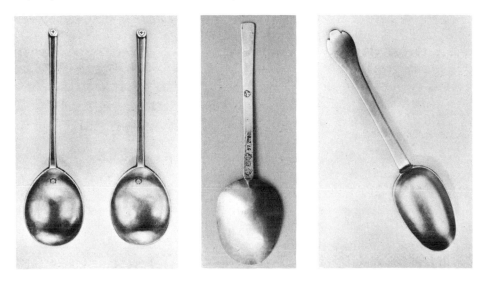

worked into coins because the Mint offered more than the market price for old wrought silver in 1697. Nevertheless, enough early Stuart silver has survived to show the skill of English silversmiths in a period in which they had little opportunity to improve their craft.

The ax that beheaded Charles I also severed the progress of English silversmithing, because Cromwell's cohorts considered plate an expression of man's vanity. However, they did approve of flat-headed spoons, the flat handles of which terminated in a skull, the bowls being engraved "Live to Die" on the front and "Die to Live" on the back.

Although silversmithing survived the austerity of the Commonwealth, the craft did not prosper under Puritan rule. But with the Restoration came an increased demand for wrought silver. Charles II and his followers had acquired a taste for lavishly ornamented plate while living at the French Court and commissioned a wide variety of articles. Meanwhile, the merchants and shopkeepers who benefited from the foreign trade resulting from Britain's exploration and colonization also patronized smith's shops. As a result, artisans were swamped with orders which in many cases they could not fill as they lacked both metal and trained assistants.

When catering to members of the Court who were anxious to possess silver equal in opulence to that they had seen at Versailles, silversmiths engaged in a riotous extravagance of decoration based on designs in Dutch pattern books. However, in their haste to finish one commission and start another, they often were guilty of inferior work. But some members of the craft—particularly Charles Shelley and Thomas Issod—produced well-proportioned, magnificently ornamented pieces during this period.

Besides creating new plate, silversmiths were kept busy replacing articles seized by pre-Restoration authorities. While some customers ordered exact duplicates of their lost treasures, others commissioned contemporary-style silver. Still others preferred a simpler decoration than the fashionable—and more expensive—repoussé ornamentation.

For customers in the latter group, silversmiths decorated plate with fluting, gadrooning, (a lobed border composed of stamped or cast convex curves, set vertically, or slanting either left or right), and acanthus leaves. The last named were often applied by the cut-card technique—after cutting and chiseling a sheet of silver into a desired pattern, the craftsman soldered it in place. The "cards" not only give the impression of relief but also strengthened a vessel raised from thin-gauge metal.

Along with plate, Restoration silversmiths produced large amounts of flatware—spoons had practically assumed their present-day shape, while three-tined forks were now common appointments on the tables of the rich—and vast numbers of mugs and tankards. Thomas Hebden of Hull and John Downwythe of Newcastle specialized in "peg tankards" which

LEFT: *Charles II plain cylindrical spout pot and cover, about 1670.* RIGHT: *Note gadroon ornamentation at the base of this bellied coffee pot, about 1770.*

derive their name from the protruding pegs that lined their interior. Tipplers wagered that they could drink the exact amount of liquid between any two pegs—a custom that is the origin of the term "to take down a peg."

Meanwhile, silversmiths were meeting the challenge of creating new types of vessels from which their patrons could serve the now fashionable tea, coffee, and chocolate, all three beverages being introduced into England in the middle of the seventeenth century. While the earliest known British-made silver coffee pot was raised by George Garthorne of London in 1681, Englishmen were patronizing coffee houses long before this date, the first being established by Cirques Jobson at Oxford in 1651.

Despite official disapproval of coffee houses—which the authorities claimed were frequented by those who spread "false, malicious, and scandalous reports to the defamation of His Majesty's Government"—and the warning of doctors that coffee would cause Englishmen to "dwindle into a succession of pygmies," coffee drinking became wide spread. As a result, silver coffee pots were in wide demand and smiths made two types: pots with curved spouts set opposite or at a right angle to the handle with a high dome for a cover; and baluster-shaped pots topped by flat covers.

London's coffee drinkers were intrigued by a notice inserted in the *Public Advertiser* for June 16, 1657:

In Bishopgate St., in Queen's Head Alley, at a Frenchman's House, is an excellent West India drink called chocolate, to be sold, where you may have it ready at any time, and also unmade at reasonable rates

The majority of those who tried the new beverage liked its taste, and not only frequented places where it was sold but also served chocolate in their own homes from silver pots. These vessels were identical to those used for coffee except that their lids had an opening for a stirrer that was used to whisk the thick liquid before it was poured.

Strangely enough, coffee and chocolate were more fashionable than "The excellent and by all Physicians approved *China* Drink called by the Chinese *Tcha*, and by other nations *Tay*, alias *Tee*" that became England's favorite beverage. Introduced about 1660, tea was primarily valued for its supposed medicinal value and was very expensive. In 1664 the East India Company presented Charles II with two pounds of tea—a royal gift as it was valued at one hundred shillings a pound. But gradually the price was reduced and those with fat purses could—as many Englishmen did—drink twenty-five cups of tea daily.

Although tea drinking became fashionable after Catherine of Braganza, wife of Charles II, began serving tea at court, only two silver teapots dated earlier than 1690 are known. One is a tall pot—now in the Victoria and Albert Museum—decorated with the arms of the East India Company and punched with the date-letter for 1670. The other vessel—prototype of all later teapots—was made in 1675. It is six inches high with a D-handle and a small S-spout set close to its Chinese wine-pot-shaped body.

Two other teapots of this type were produced by Richard Hoare and Benjamin Pyne about 1690. Pyne was one of the great silversmiths of the

RIGHT: *Richard Williams fashioned this chocolate pot which has unusual card work behind the spout and handle sockets. Note the small hinged lid on the main lid through which the handle of the stirring stick extended.* BELOW: *Bullet teapot dated 1722, the work of Humphrey Payne.*

*Front and side views of a silvergilt ewer by Pierre Harache, 1697 or 1703.*

late seventeenth and early eighteenth centuries and, whether ornamenting hexagonal dishes with lavish chasing and embossing, casting candlesticks, fashioning silver andirons, or raising vessels, had few peers.

Along with competing with such outstanding native artisans as George and Francis Garthorne, Benjamin Bathhurst, John Fawdery, and Humphrey Payne, Pyne had to contend with the clever craftsmanship of Huguenot silversmiths who had fled to England following the revocation of the Edict of Nantes in 1685. Actually, French metal workers had been crossing the Channel for some years previously, not only to avoid religious persecution but also because of Louis XIV's laws restricting silversmithing. At first, these refugees were welcomed by English craftsmen who had turned from Dutch to French pattern books and could profitably employ the designing skill and refined techniques of the immigrants in producing wares in the new style.

But hospitality turned to hostility when the French smiths requested that their marks be registered at Goldsmiths' Hall. Jealous of the newcomers—whose ability was forcing them to improve the quality of their work—members of the Goldsmiths' Guild paid little attention to such petitions but did listen to the protests of John Boddington, John Brace, Isaac Deighton, William Fawdery, Richard Syng, and Joseph Ward who were against "certain Frenchmen becoming free of the city."

Unable to register their punches or to have their work assayed, the refugees were either forced to sell their unmarked silver at low prices or to work for registered smiths who stamped their creations with their own marks. The latter practice became so widespread that eventually the Goldsmiths' Company forbade members of the guild to buy plate from "Necessitous strangers whose desperate fortunes obliged them to work at miserable rates."

The first Huguenot silversmith to receive his Freedom—the recognition of a craftsman by a guild and permission to work under its jurisdiction—

was Pierre Harache. His certificate, dated 1682, stated that he had "lately come from France for to avoid persecution and live quietly." A master craftsman, Harache fashioned silver wine bottles, pierced castor sets, candlesticks with plain baluster stems mounted on circular or octagonal feet, George II's christening basin, spoons, and a wide variety of plate. Harache delighted in producing ornately decorated plate and continued to fashion it after both his fellow exiles and such native experts in the art of embossing as Robert Trimbell, John Boddington, and Timothy Ley discarded elaboration for delicate decorations that contrasted with large areas of highly polished metal. At the end of Queen Anne's reign, the trend toward restrained ornamentation became more pronounced and, by the 1720's, fashion demanded that plate be severely plain. While Harache favored the baroque style, he did create pieces in the new manner, employing Simon Griblein, one of the finest of eighteenth-century engravers, to do the chasing.

The shift to simply decorated silver was due to a shortage in metal. At first silversmiths secured enough silver by melting down coins, but the passage of an "Act for encouraging the bringing in of wrought plate to be coined" in 1697 ended the practice. By its provisions, plate could be melted into coinage because it was of sterling standard, but all new plate had to be fashioned by a new standard of purity. This was the Britannia standard—958 per thousand pure—and smiths were ordered to hallmark wares fashioned from it with punches showing Britannia seated and a lion's head erased. The law also specified that silversmiths reregister their personal marks and limited them to using only the first two initials of their surnames. While this was annoying, the craft had more serious concerns: the new standard made wrought silver more expensive and this could reduce the number of commissions they received; and many craftsmen wondered if, after working relatively hard sterling, they could master the softer and more malleable Britannia.

Their fears were groundless. Between March 1697 and June 1720 when the high standard became obligatory—it is still legal and occasionally used —English silversmiths produced some of their finest work. Moreover, they had all the commissions they could handle, ranging from orders for ceremonial plate to a wide variety of domestic silver including beverage pots, spice boxes, trays, and tea canisters. As tea was usually blended at the table to please individual taste, silversmiths supplied canisters in sets. Like all domestic silver they changed shape to meet the demands of fashion—the undecorated oblong canisters of the Queen Anne and George I era gave way to round-shouldered oblong or square ones in the 1730's, and these in turn were replaced by vase-shaped canisters in the next decade. In fact, it is doubtful if Seth Lofthouse—a silver warming pan bearing his touch is in

*Severely simple Queen Anne cof-
fee pot by John Folkingham and
tea caddy bearing Andrew Raven's
hallmark.*

Buckingham Palace—who made a small tea canister in 1703 shaped like a
bottle and ornamented with chinoiserie scenes, visualized that fifty years
later, Samuel Taylor would be specializing in bombé canister sets covered
all over with rococo decorations.

Strangely enough, just as canisters underwent a change in shape, so did
their name. About 1790, the word canister gave way to caddy. This word
is derived from the Malayan *kati*, the weight by which tea was sold. *Kati*
was first corrupted into case, and then became caddy.

Silversmiths created spoons for the specific purpose of removing tea
from caddies. These often had fancifully shaped bowls representing fish,
fans, shells, paws, jockey caps, and other objects. The two hundred different types of caddy spoons displayed at the Victoria and Albert Museum in
London offer proof that in designing them silversmiths gave free rein to
their imaginations and devoted as much skill to making them as they did
when fashioning larger and more profitable wares.

"All well-regulated families," Addison wrote in 1711, "set apart an hour
every morning for tea, bread, and butter." By the end of Queen Anne's
reign, Englishmen were taking milk and sugar with their tea and silversmiths supplied the suitable vessels with which to serve them. Harache is
responsible for the helmet-shaped ewers with delicate, applied decorations
duplicated by other craftsmen, including his fellow Huguenots David

LEFT: *Helmet-shaped cream ewer made by Thomas Law of Sheffield.* RIGHT: *Heavily chased cream ewer decorated with pastoral scenes.*

Willaume and Pierre Platel—the latter fashioning one of gold. Another craftsman, Simon Pantin, who created part of a service for the Empress of Russia, added to tea-table equipage with his silver spirit lamp to boil water at the table, while Peter Archambo, who had learned his craft in France, raised globular tea kettles.

Huguenot artisans did not limit their talents to appointments for the tea table. Their ornately decorated plate was popular with the wealthy; their twenty- or thirty-piece toilet sets delighted ladies of fashion, while their wine coolers were highly approved of by gentlemen who boasted of their knowledge of vintages. Although Huguenot smiths received few commissions for tankards and mugs, they did, along with such native smiths as Philip Rolles and Gabriel Sleath, fashion wine cisterns (large oval bowls which were filled with water and ice to cool bottled wine) and wine fountains (vase-shaped covered vessels with taps).

The largest piece of silver known to be wrought by an English silversmith was a wine cistern commissioned by Parliament and raffled off to pay the cost of a bridge across the Thames at Westminster. Designed by Henry Jernegan and raised by Charles Kandler in 1734, it held sixty gallons, weighed nearly 8,000 ounces, was 5½ feet long, and 3½ feet wide. Four chained leopards supported the bowl which rose from a bed of acanthus leaves; boys and satyrs were depicted on the side panels; festoons of vines bearing grapes encircled the rim; the handles were formed by nude demi-figures of a man and a woman holding bunches of grapes. Eventually, this massive example of the silversmith's art was acquired by the traditional "unnamed buyer," but the chances are that the purchaser was Catherine II of Russia—an avid silver collector—because the cistern became a prized possession of the Tzars.

The barbaric splendor of Kandler's cistern was never equaled by the smiths who fashioned punch bowls. Punch—the word is supposedly derived from the Hindustani *paunch* meaning "five" because the recipe for the beverage called for five components: spirits, lemon juice, sugar, spices, and water—was served in three types of bowls. Some were merely hemispherical containers similar to the porcelain ones then being imported from the Orient and were simply chased. Others were more elaborately ornamented—the result of Huguenot influence. Still others, such as the one made by Robert Cooper in 1691, combined both styles.

Certain late-seventeenth and early-eighteenth century punch bowls had notched, demountable silver rims on which glasses could be hung. Known as monteiths, these bowls owe their name to the notches on the bottom of the cloak of "a fantastical Scot called Monsieur Monteigh" who was famous at Oxford for his ability to mix punch.

The roster of master smiths in England during the eighteenth century is a long one. However, a number of them are as anonymous as the artisan "justly acclaimed as the finest craftsman of the mid seventeenth century" who is known only by his punch—a "hound sejant." This is particularly true of Huguenot craftsmen who lacked the money to register their marks after the Goldsmiths' Company opened its membership to French-trained silversmiths and were forced to work for native-born masters who took

Left: *Silvergilt bowl and cover by Philip Rolles, 1710, bearing the Royal Arms of Queen Anne.* Right: *Oblong inkstand by Philip Rolles, 1716.*

*Monteith decorated on rim with chased cherub heads and scroll work, the body embossed.*

the credit for their creations. Moreover, while there are lengthy lists of both hallmarks and craftsmen, it is often impossible to link the two. Nevertheless, a tremendous amount of eighteenth-century silver can be positively attributed to certain individuals. In some cases, the style of a piece and the technique used to fashion it reveal the name of the master who created it; in others, makers can be identified by the hallmarks they reregistered when the sterling standard was restored in 1720.

The styles of the plate on which these punches appear—many of the reregistered hallmarks were identical with those employed before 1679—show the versatility of British silversmiths of the eighteenth century. Always conscious of changing public taste, they wrought in turn undecorated plate, a blend of the plain and fanciful, baroque, rococo, and the classical designs made popular by architect Robert Adam.

It is impossible in a book of this size to do more than list a few of the outstanding craftsmen who worked in London and the provinces during the eighteenth century. Among the latter were several generations of the Richardson and Pemberton families in Chester; Exeter's Pentecost Symonds, John Avery, John March, and John Elston; and the artisans at Newcastle-upon-Tyne. The last named formed their own company in 1720, having been united with Newcastle's glaziers, pewterers, and plumbers since 1536, and, in the years that followed, Thomas Partis, Isaac Cookson, James Kirkup, William Robertson, and Robert Makepeace, along with others, made Newcastle a famous silver center.

Not only were all these men outstanding craftsmen but also some were prominent citizens in their communities. For example, in Chester, several members of the Richardson family served as aldermen, mayors, and sheriffs. However, some members of the craft in York were equally well known for breaking the law because they made substandard plate. The Goldsmiths' Company investigated charges against Thomas Mangy, while another member of this large family of smiths, Arthur Mangy, was hanged for clipping and forging coinage.

Among the men who dominated the craft of silversmithing in London during the first half of the eighteenth century, then, were: Peter Archambo, Augustine Courtauld, William Cripps, Paul Crispin, George and Francis Garthorne, Paul Goode, Pierre Harache, John and Simon Le Sage, Isaac Liger, Lewis Mettayer, Anthony and Francis Nelme, Simon Pantin, Humphrey Payne, Pierre Platel, Benjamin Pyne, Isaac Ribouleau, William Scarlett, David Tanquerey, George Wickes, and David Willaume. However, while all these men—and many of their contemporaries—created flat and hollow wares that show they were masters of form and ornament, none was the equal of Paul De Lamerie.

RIGHT: *Teapot by Pentecost Symonds of Exeter. Pieces by this master smith are very rare.* BELOW LEFT: *Ship-engraved punch bowl by R. Makepiece and F. Batty of Newcastle, 1719.* BELOW RIGHT: *George Wickes gilt bowl with fluting and applied shell and scroll work.*

The son of French Huguenots—Paul Souchay de la Merie and Constance Le Roux—who had fled from France, Paul was born in 1688 in the Netherlands where his father served as an army captain. Three years later the family moved to London. While the captain could afford the taxes on their house in Berwick Street, he had far more pride than wealth—although he accepted a small pension from the English government in 1701—and, considering himself an aristocrat, refused to learn a trade.

However, in 1703—the same year both father and son were granted English citizenship by Letters of Denization—he agreed to Paul's becoming indentured to "Peter Plattel, Citizen and Goldsmith of London for the term of seven years." It is possible that Platel was a friend of the family and persuaded Captain de la Merie that there was nothing ignoble in being a silversmith. On the other hand, Platel, who had come to England in the

RIGHT: *Philip Rolles made these candlesticks in 1699-1700.*

BELOW: *Two examples of De Lamerie's skill: a rococo ewer made in 1742 and a plain oval fluted dish dated 1746.*

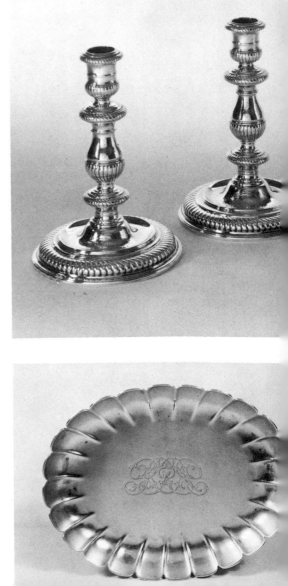

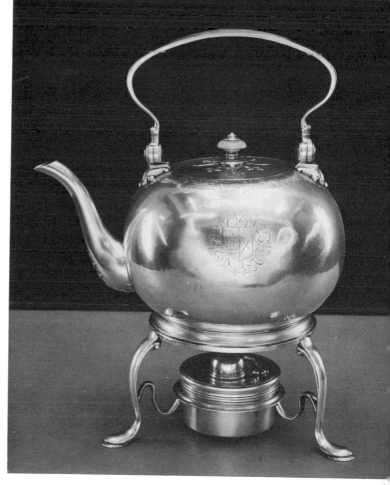

*Spirit lamp, stand, and kettle with card work applied to the lid and spout, by Anthony Nelme.*

train of William III, might merely have accepted Paul as an apprentice as a kindly gesture toward fellow Huguenots who needed assistance. At any rate, he did not demand the customary fee from Paul.

De Lamerie could not have had a better teacher. Platel, who had received his freedom in 1699, wrought magnificent gold plate for the nobility that patronized his Pall Mall shop. Under his supervision, Paul developed into an excellent craftsman, acquiring an uncanny knowledge of what could or could not be done with metal of Britannia standard during the years of his apprenticeship.

After learning all that Platel could teach and working as a journeyman, Paul De Lamerie (he always used the capital "D") entered his first mark, LA crowned, in the register at Goldsmiths' Hall and opened a shop in Windmill Street near the Hay Market. At first he fashioned wares with restrained ornamentation—a characteristic of most of the smiths who worked with the softer Britannia standard during the Queen Anne and early Georgian Periods. But within a short time he broke away from his fellow craftsmen who were content to achieve effect by subordinating

*Silver cake basket by Paul De Lamerie, 1745-1746.*

decoration to the play of light and shade on the curves of their creations and boldly employed gadroon borders, diapers—patterns formed by the continuous repetition of a design—piercing, engraving, flat chasing, and applied details.

Although many of his applied castings and piercings were standard patterns taken from such books as Gibelin's *Book of Ornaments useful to all Artists,* De Lamerie gave them a quality all of his own. Moreover, he had no scruples about duplicating motifs if he thought they suited his purpose. Nor did he hesitate to borrow the designs of other smiths, both of his own time and of the past—but none of those who attempted to duplicate his workmanship during the forty years he practiced his craft succeeded.

A master at combining function and beauty, De Lamerie's work brought him so many customers that within five years of receiving his Freedom he was able to buy another house in Windmill Street and marry Louise Juliott, daughter of an important Huguenot family. In 1717 he was admitted to the Livery of the Goldsmiths' Company but he had no time to celebrate. Between commissions and retail sales he was far too busy at the *Golden Ball* —the name by which his shop was known.

Equally talented whether turning out well-portioned beverage pots, baluster-shaped candlesticks, dishes and bowls ornamented with engraving or flat chasing, or richly decorated massive pieces, De Lamerie never fashioned plate that was not flawless in execution. He devoted as much care to raising a simply chased teakettle to which a wicker handle was lapped—his handles were applied by Scotts of London who still do this work for contemporary silversmiths—as he did when fashioning an ornately chased wine cistern.

Recognizing no limit to his skill, De Lamerie continued to work Brittannia after 1720 when his fellow craftsmen took advantage of the repeal of the Act of 1697 and returned to the sterling standard. From the *Golden Ball* came two-handled cups and covers (elaborately ornamented or delicately chased depending on a client's taste): toilet services bearing exquisite strapwork; baluster-stemmed candlesticks; tea caddies decorated by the repoussé technique; and trays and salvers of exceptional beauty.

De Lamerie fashioned one of his finest salvers for Robert Walpole. As was customary, Walpole, upon retiring as chancellor of the exchequer in 1728, was allowed to keep the defaced seal of his office. Walpole commissioned De Lamerie to make a salver from his seal and, with the aid of William Hogarth, one of the greatest of English engravers who had been apprenticed to silversmith Ellis Gamble, De Lamerie created a masterpiece. Hogarth, incidentally, is also credited with doing other engraving for De Lamerie but none of this work has been positively identified.

Meanwhile, De Lamerie was finding inspiration in the rococo style that had been introduced into France at the beginning of the eighteenth century. Rococo—the word is derived from the French *rocaille*, "pebble work" —is a florid style, its characteristics being asymmetrical curves, foliage, scrolls, shells, and piercing. Yet, despite his adoption of rococoism—a style that was to dominate English silversmithing of the 1740's—De Lamerie "knew infallibly when to leave surfaces plain and how far his glorious decorative detail should extend." As a result, he contrasted flat chasing with decorative motifs as often as he completely covered a ware with applied shells, masks, diaper and floral designs.

However, as he pioneered in the rococo style, De Lamerie came to the conclusion that, being harder, sterling was a more suitable metal than Britannia for creating highly ornamented silver. Therefore, in 1732, he registered the mark, PL crowned, as his punch for working in sterling.

By now De Lamerie's reputation had spread beyond England and he was commissioned by the Russian Government to make two silver chandeliers for the Kremlin. Each of the chandeliers he produced had sixteen branches —those on one being in two tiers—and both were covered with acanthus leaves, masks, and strapwork surmounted by the Imperial Crown. Lavish as these chandeliers were, the centerpiece De Lamerie created for a Russian count made them seem simple by comparison.

While De Lamerie had every reason to be proud of these foreign commissions, he received an even greater honor at home in 1734 when the Goldsmiths' Company asked him to make some plate for its collection. Seven years later De Lamerie delivered to Goldsmiths' Hall the ewer and basin that give lasting evidence of his inventiveness, mastery of decoration, and craftsmanship.

During the years that followed, De Lamerie fashioned a wide variety of silver ranging from tureens (named for Marshal Tureen of France who used his helmet as a soup bowl in the field) to cumbersome centerpieces which, being designed for ornamentation rather than use, enabled him to engage in riotous rococoism. However, busy as he was in the shop, he found time for his wife and three daughters—his sons had died in childhood —and to rise to the rank of major in the army, along with serving successively as Fourth, Third, and Second Warden of the Goldsmiths' Company.

As the first half of the eighteenth century ended, De Lamerie, who had employed rococoism for more than a decade before it became popular, gradually abandoned it. He had always delighted in chasing plain surfaces and, weary from creating flamboyant designs, returned to the ornamentation he had used so successfully at the start of his career.

Possibly De Lamerie, who had been responsible for the acceptance of the rococo style in England, could have influenced his fellow craftsmen to join in a revival of the simple silver of the early Georgian Period. However, such speculation is idle for Paul De Lamerie, one of the greatest silversmiths of all times, died in August, 1751.

While De Lamerie and other leaders of the craft had journeymen and apprentices to assist them, less successful artisans relied on the help of their wives. Often, upon her husband's death, a smith's widow would continue his business and, if she had worked with him for at least seven years, was permitted to register her mark—which was enclosed by a distinctive panel signifying her status—at Goldsmiths' Hall.

Although only advanced collectors have any knowledge of Sarah Parr, Hester Fawdery, Ann Tanquery, Mary Johnson, Edith Fletcher, Elizabeth Goodwin, and the other women silversmiths of the eighteenth century, even the novice has heard of Hester Bateman, one of the most celebrated figures in the history of English silversmithing.

In 1730, twenty-year-old Hester Needham married John Bateman, an "outworker" who made silverware for other craftsmen in his home. After fourteen years of work, the Batemans accumulated enough money to purchase a combination house and shop on Bunhill Road. Hester probably made

the decision to buy the property, which was just outside London's northern boundary. A shrewd businesswoman—although unable to read or write—she would be quick to see the advantage of a shop outside London where guild regulations did not apply, for John was an unregistered smith.

There was little that strong-willed, energetic Hester did not know about silversmithing, because in addition to keeping house and raising six children, she had worked beside her husband most of her married life. Her first chore had been to hand-burnish articles to give them a soft luster, a tedious task but one that gave Hester a feel for metal so that she soon developed into a master craftsman.

When John died in 1760 he left Hester his tools—a bequest that confirms her skill, as an artisan's tools were his most prized possession and he "never would entrust them, even after his death, to anyone incapable of using them with a skill less equal to his own."

Actually, Bateman's tools comprised the greater part of his estate as his business was a small one. Determined to keep it operating and, if possible, expand it, Hester, at the age of fifty-one, registered her mark, HB in script, at Goldsmiths' Hall.

Despite the competition of Cornelius Bland, James Hoewell, and the other smiths dwelling on Bunhill Road, Hester managed to retain her husband's clients and to secure new ones. However, most of her customers stamped her creations with their own marks or overstamped Hester's punch. This annoyed Hester, but lacking capital she was forced to work the metal

*A silver spoon by Peter and William Bateman.*

of others who wished to give the impression that they made all the wares sold in their shops.

Hester did not work alone, being assisted by her eldest son John, who had received his Freedom in 1751 after serving his apprenticeship with William Shaw, and by John Linney. The latter had been indentured to Hester's husband and, by recognized custom, was working out his time with his dead master's widow. When Hester's sons Peter and Jonathan completed their apprenticeship to Richard Clarke, a successful silversmith who had married their sister Letticia, they also joined their mother at Bunhill Road where the Batemans were to make silver for one hundred years.

Although Hester designed and supervised the making of all silver that bears her punch, much of it was the work of her children. However, whether a piece was made by Hester, her sons, grandsons, or Jonathan's wife Ann (the daughter of a Huguenot family related to silversmiths serving the French Court), their creations have a characteristic elegance that makes Bateman silver easy to identify.

All Bateman silver features simplicity of form and flow of line. Most of the shop's early domestic silver—which was its specialty—is sparsely decorated, the commonest ornamentation being a beaded border along the edges of serving pieces and around the tops of hollow wares. Hester also used beads to conceal seams such as the join where the stem of a goblet attached to the bowl. Occasionally, she designed a piece that called for gadrooning and, toward the end of her career, frequently substituted her favorite bead motif for a thread decoration.

In the early 1770's, Hester expanded her activities and began accepting commissions as well as continuing to serve other smiths as an outworker. She was encouraged to do so by Sir James Easdaile, banker, onetime Lord Mayor of London and a friendly neighbor of the Batemans. Easdaile ordered several pieces from Hester and it is likely that one or two were beer mugs, for Sir James had designed his residence so that one of its doors opened directly into an adjoining alehouse.

Although Hester was grateful to Sir James for his patronage, she had no intention of catering to the wealthy. Always hardheaded in business matters, she realized that despite the development of Sheffield Plate—which had covered English tables with rich-looking but inexpensive silverware—many middle-class families of taste preferred honestly priced, well-made, sterling silver to articles fashioned from silver overlaying copper.

Therefore, she specialized in domestic silver: castors, coasters (used by the gentlemen to slide bottles along the table when the ladies retired to the drawing room after dinner and the cloth was removed), cream jugs, salts, spoons, sugar bowls, and beverage services. Strangely enough, while the Batemans created "useful" silver, there is no record of a candlestick or a candelabra bearing their marks.

The high quality of Bateman workmanship and Hester's determination not only enabled the shop to compete with the products of Sheffield and Birmingham—which were driving many silversmiths into bankruptcy—but also to show large profits. By 1786, the business had outgrown the facilities at 107 Bunhill Road and the Batemans purchased the house on either side. Shortly afterward, the taxes were raised on the property and Hester, in typical fashion, demanded and received an abatement.

Besides making domestic silver, Hester also fashioned a wand of office for the verger of St. Paul's Cathedral, bells of many types, dozens of medallions and medals, gauntlets for the queen's ladies-in-waiting, and other articles. Her hallmark also appears on ecclesiastical plate and several presentation pieces. Among the latter are an oval salver engraved with a view of the Town Hall in Lancaster, an ogee-shaped punch bowl bearing the arms of the City of Chester, a pair of cups for the Corporation of Hull, and plate

*White overlay glass and Sheffield stand.*

*Matthew Boulton of Birmingham made these wine coolers with lion-mask, loose-ring handles in 1801.*

for the Coopers', Grocers', and Needlemakers' Companies.

In 1790, Hester celebrated her eighty-first birthday by announcing her retirement. It had not been an easy decision because she was still alert, active, and vigorous, but she realized that Peter and Jonathan were capable of continuing the business and seeing that her grandsons were properly trained to succeed them. After having Peter draw up her will, in which she specified that her executors would receive their fees *after* all its bequests were made, Hester left Bunhill Road and went to live with the widowed Letticia. Although Letticia did everything possible to make her mother happy, Hester missed the routine of the shop and began to fail, and, on September 26, 1794, death came to England's most famous woman silversmith.

Peter now assumed charge of the shop. He was assisted by Ann (Jonathan had died in 1791), her son William, and his nephew Jonathan II (whose skill never equaled that of others of his family). However, Ann was an exceptionally clever craftsman and employed Hester's thread ornamentation most effectively. Moreover, Ann had many of her mother-in-law's characteristics. Recognizing Ann's business acumen as well as her skill, Peter, after registering their joint mark, PB-AB, changed the name of the firm to Ann Bateman and Company.

In 1825, Peter retired at the age of eighty-five. William inherited the shop and most of Peter's fortune, his uncle leaving but small sums to his other nephews and nieces "as they had borrowed from me in my lifetime double or treble the amount they would otherwise have received at my decease."

Williams' designs were Victorian at its worst, but his craftsmanship was typically Bateman. While his grandmother had suffered the indignity of having her mark overstamped, William rose to be Prime Warden of the Goldsmiths' Company. Upon his death in 1850, his son William II, a competent silversmith, took over the firm but broke family tradition by entering into a partnership with an artisan not connected by blood or marriage. Although this alliance did not last very long, it marked the last chapter in the history of the Bateman dynasty of silversmiths.

By the time William Bateman II was working at his bench more people were purchasing Sheffield Plate than hand-wrought silver. The knowledge that a thin sheet of silver could be fused to a thicker sheet of copper and that the combination could be used as a single metal had been accidentally discovered by Thomas Bouslover while repairing a knife. Bouslover had employed his discovery to make buttons, buckles, and boxes, but he abandoned it because of financial difficulties. However, Matthew Boulton of Birmingham, using die stamping, presses, and other machinery, mass-produced a wide variety of inexpensive wares from the new alloy by 1765.

Conservative silversmiths—and their patrons—sneered at Boulton's products and derisively called everything made in Birmingham "Brummagen"—

*J. Wakelin and R. Garrard fashioned this oval teapot and stand of Adam design.*

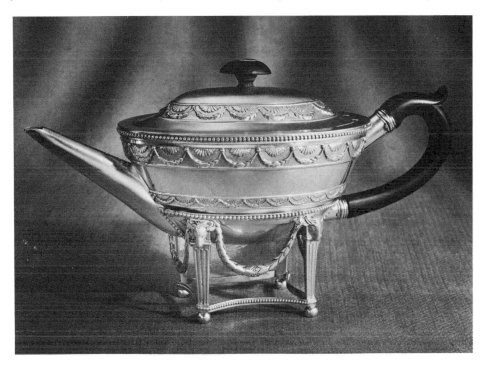

after a worthless copper coin said to have been counterfeited there. But they could not deny that Thomas Law, Henry Tudor, and the other artisans who cast Boulton's dies were enabling him to duplicate the neo-classical style that dominated English silversmithing between 1760 and 1790.

While Robert Adam, the architect and prime proponent of neo-classicism, never worked directly with a silversmith, he supplied designs for plate to patrons. These, in turn, passed Adams' sketches on to their favorite craftsman. Actually, Adams' influence could be seen in most London silver shops: John Carter, Louisa Courtauld, George Cowles, Andrew Fogelberg, Stephen Gilbert, Frederick Kandler, Robert Sharp, Daniel Smith, James Young and others drew upon "the beautiful spirit of antiquity." As a result, these smiths adapted the shape of Grecian urns to race trophies and sideboard pieces, used the column as a basis for candlesticks, and ornamented their work with classical motifs.

To achieve the lightness and delicacy advocated by Adam, silversmiths employed piercing and bright-cut engraving. Among the masters of the latter technique was John Schofield, a specialist in cruets who effectively contrasted the play of light from the hundreds of tiny facets he engraved against plain polished surfaces.

While many smiths dealt directly with customers, others supplied neo-classical wares to those craftsmen who operated large retail shops such as the one owned by Parker and Wakelin, a firm that eventually became Garrard & Company, the present-day Crown Jewelers. Parker and Wakelin only accepted wares made by outstanding artisans who frequently worked for them exclusively as did Sebastian and James Crispin, masters of the Adam style, and Thomas Pitts who supplied them with epergnes.

The Adam style lost its popularity as the eighteenth century drew to a close and silver once again became ornate. However, smiths still relied on ancient civilizations to provide ideas for ornamentation and they now blended the Sphinx of Egypt, Greek palmettes, and Roman masks. Borrowing from Wedgwood—which was unusual, for potters drew their forms and decorations from silversmiths—Andrew Fogelberg and Stephen Gilbert catered to the new fashion by applying Tassie's paste reproductions of engraved gem stones to their wares. At the same time, Philip Rundell and John Bridge were commissioning leading artists and sculptors to design plate bearing modeled figures which were executed by Digby Scott and Benjamin Smith.

The demand for presentation plate to reward Nelson, Wellington, and the other military and naval leaders who had defeated Napoleon marked an end of neo-classicism. Turning again to rococo, smiths revived the lavish ornamentation of De Lamerie or engaged in flights of fancy. Some of the pieces they produced in the latter mood are charming—the cheese dish with

ABOVE: *These sauce tureens with reeded loop handles, beaded rim banding, foliated dome covers with a pomegranate finial, and decorated in repoussé with bowknotted drapery, swags, and spiral flutes are the work of Louisa Courtauld and George Cowles.*

RIGHT: *Tea urn with fluted decorations made by John Schofield.*

a mouse in each corner warily eyeing a finial formed like a trap fashioned by John Moore in 1804; honey jars in the form of hives; and creamers shaped like cows. While John Schuppe is credited with raising many of these creamers, they did not originate with him. The first had been designed by Nicholas Sprimont nearly a century earlier before he abandoned silver-

*Centerpiece wrought by John Parker and Edward Wakelin weighing 630 ounces shows the lavish tableware of the time of George III.*

LEFT: *An outstanding example of Paul Storr's craftsmanship—a tea urn made in 1809.*

OPPOSITE: *Silversmithing has survived the machine age in England—a set of silver models of the Household Brigade, presented to Elizabeth II in 1953 on the occasion of her Coronation.*

smithing to manage the Chelsea porcelain works.

But while the unusual found a ready market, the greatest demand was for magnificent plate. Strangely enough, the smith who supplied the most outstanding had served his apprenticeship in the Adam era and, in the early days of his career, fashioned neo-classical silver. Recognized as one of the greatest silversmiths of all times, Paul Storr did much of his finest work for Rundell and Bridge who utilized to the fullest his talent for decoration and proportion.

However, Storr had little chance to display his skill in design, for Rundell and Bridge insisted that he follow the designs supplied them by John Flaxman and other leading artists. This was frustrating but, what was worse, Storr and Rundell were incompatible. Finally, Storr was able to dissolve his arrangement with Rundell and Bridge and opened his own shop where he made extravagantly ornamented plate or plain pieces depending upon his mood. But no matter what he created, his silver was correct and perfect in every detail.

When Storr retired in 1839, the roar of the machine was becoming heard over the hammers of the craftsman. The roar grew louder in the 1840's when inexpensive Sheffield Plate was priced out of the market by wares mass-produced by the new process of plating silver electrochemically. Nevertheless, silversmithing has survived the machine age in England, just as the craft withstood the religious reforms and wars of earlier times. Today, steeped in the ancient traditions of their craft, Alex Styles and other English silversmiths are creating ceremonial, commemorative, and domestic silver that would win the approval of all their predecessors, including good Saint Dunstan.

# Selected Bibliography

———⊰⊱———

A listing of all the sources consulted in the preparation of this volume would fill dozens of pages. Therefore, only those titles that have been particularly helpful to the author—and which should be equally useful to the tyro-collector who wishes to know more about the crafts and craftsmen dealt with—have been included. The attention of the reader who desires more specific information about a particular artisan, period, or style is directed to the bibliographies in the books listed below and to the *Reader's Guide to Periodical Literature* which indexes articles that have appeared in magazines dealing with antiques and art. Not only is the author indebted to the specialists who wrote these articles but also to those responsible for various museum bulletins, newspaper articles, and privately printed monographs.

## FURNITURE

Bell, J. M. (editor). *The Furniture Designs of Chippendale, Hepplewhite and Sheraton.* New York: McBride, 1938.

Brackett, Oliver. *Thomas Chippendale: A Study of His Life, Work and Influence.* London: Hodder & Stoughton, 1924.

Cescinsky, N. and Gribble, E. R. *Early English Furniture and Woodwork.* 2 vols. London: Routledge, 1922.

Chippendale, Thomas. *The Gentleman and Cabinet-Maker's Director.* London, 1754.

Clouston, R. S. *English Furniture and Furniture Makers of the Eighteenth Century.* London: Hurst & Blockett, 1906.

Edwards, Ralph. *Sheraton Furniture Designs.* London: Tiranti, Ltd., 1946.

———. *Hepplewhite Furniture Designs.* London: Tiranti, Ltd., 1947.

——— and Jourdain, Margaret. *Georgian Cabinet-Makers.* London: Country Life, 1946.

Fastnedge, R. *English Literature Styles from 1500 to 1830.* Los Angeles: Jenkins, 1961.

Gloag, John. *English Furniture.* Fourth edition. London: A. & C. Black, 1951.

———. *The Englishman's Chair: Origins, Design, and Social History of Seat Furniture in England.* London: Allen, 1954.

———. *A Short Dictionary of Furniture.* New York: Holt, Rinehart and Winston, 1965.

Hepplewhite, A. & Co. *The Cabinet-Maker and Upholsterer's Guide,* or *Repository of Designs for Every Article of Household Furniture.* London: 1788.

Hughes, Therle. *Old English Furniture.* New York: Macmillan, 1964.

Jourdain, Margaret. *English Decoration and Furniture of the Later Eighteenth Century (1760-1803).* London: Batsford, 1922.

———. *English Interiors in Smaller Houses from the Restoration to the Regency (1660-1830).* New York: Scribner's, 1923.

———. *English Decoration and Furniture of the Early Renaissance (1500-1650).* New York: Scribner's, 1926.

———. *Regency Furniture (1795-1820).* London: Country Life, 1948.

Joy, E. T. *English Furniture* A.D. *43-1950.* London: Batsford, 1962.

Macquoid, Percy. *A History of English Furniture.* 4 vols. London: Lawrence and Bullen, 1904-1908.

——— and Edwards, Ralph. *The Dictionary of English Furniture.* 3 vols. London: Country Life, 1924-1927.

Nickerson, David. *English Furniture of the Eighteenth Century.* New York: Putnam, 1963.

Roe, Fred. *Ancient Coffers and Cupboards.* London: Methuen & Co., 1902.

———. *Old Oak Furniture.* London: Methuen & Co., 1905.

Sheraton, Thomas. *The Cabinet-Maker and Upholsterer's Drawing Book.* London: 1791-1793.

Symonds, R. W. *English Furniture from Charles II to George II.* New York: International Studio, 1929.

———. *Chippendale Furniture Designs.* London: Tiranti, Ltd., 1941.

———. *Veneered Walnut Furniture (1660-1760).* London: Tiranti, Ltd., 1946.

———. *Furniture Making in Seventeenth and Eighteenth Century England.* London: National Magazine Co., 1955.

## GLASS

Ash, D. *How to Identify English Drinking Glasses and Decanters.* London: Bell, 1962.

Bedford, John. *Bristol and Other Coloured Glass.* New York: Walker, 1965.

Bles, J. *Rare English Glasses of the XVII and XVIII Centuries.* Boston: Houghton, Mifflin, 1925.

Buckley, W. *Diamond Engraved Glasses of the Sixteenth Century.* London: Benn, 1929.

Elville, E. M. *The Collector's Dictionary of Glass.* London: Country Life, 1961.

———. *English and Irish Cut Glass, 1750-1950.* New York: Taplinger, 1962.

———. *English Tableglass.* New York: Taplinger, 1963.

Fleming, J. A. *Scottish and Jacobite Glass.* Glasgow: Jackson, 1938.

Honey, William B. *English Glass.* London: Collins, 1946.

Loewenthal, L. *Georgian Glass Pictures and Needlework.* London: Mitre Press, 1934.

Thorpe, W. A. *English Glass.* Third edition. London: A. & C. Black, 1961.

Wakefield, Hugh. *Nineteenth Century British Glass.* New York: Yoseloff, 1962.

## POTTERY AND PORCELAIN

Barnard, Harry. *Chats on Wedgwood Ware.* London: Unwin, 1924.

Bedford, John. *Staffordshire Pottery Figures.* New York: Walker, 1965.

Blacker, J. *The ABC of English Salt-Glaze Stoneware from Dwight to Doulton.* London: Paul, 1922.

Blunt, Reginald. *Cheyne Book of Chelsea*

*China*. Boston: Houghton-Mifflin, 1925.

Bryant, G. E. *Chelsea Porcelain Toys*. London: Medici, 1925.

Cannon, T. G. *Old Spode*. London: Lourie, 1924.

Cox, W. E. *Book of Pottery and Porcelain*. 2 vols. New York: Crown, 1944.

Fisher, S. *British Pottery and Porcelain*. New York: Arco, 1962.

Gardner, F. H. *English Delftware*. New York: Van Nostrand, 1948.

Godden, G. A. *British Pottery and Porcelain 1780-1850*. Toronto: Ryerson, 1964.

———. *An Illustrated Encyclopedia of British Pottery and Porcelain*. New York: Crown, 1966.

Gorley, Jean. *Wedgwood*. New York: Barrows, 1950.

Haggar, R. G. *English Pottery Figures 1660-1860*. London: Tiranti, 1967.

Hughes, G. B. and Hughes, T. *English Porcelain and Bone China*. New York: Macmillan, 1961.

Hurlbutt, Frank. *Bow Porcelain*. London: Bell, 1926.

———. *Bristol Porcelain*. London: Bell, 1928.

———. *Old Derby Porcelain and its Artist-Workmen*. London: Laurie, 1928.

———. *Chelsea China*. Liverpool University Press, 1937.

Lane, A. *English Porcelain Figures of the Eighteenth Century*. New York: Yoseloff, 1961.

Mackenna, F. Severne. *Cookworthy's Plymouth and Bristol Porcelain*. Leigh-on-Sea: Lewis, 1945.

Mankowitz, Wolf. *Wedgwood*. London: Batsford, 1953.

Price, E. J. *Astbury, Whieldon, and Ralph Wood Figures, and Toby Jugs*. London: Bodley Head, 1922.

Savage, George. *Porcelain Through the Ages*. London: Cassell, 1961.

———. *English Pottery and Porcelain*. London: Oldbourne, 1961.

Stanley, Louis. *Collecting Staffordshire Pottery*. Garden City: Doubleday, 1963.

Wykes-Joyce, Max. *7000 Years of Pottery and Porcelain*. New York: Philosophical, 1958.

## SILVER

Ash, D. *How to Identify English Silver Drinking Vessels 630-1830*. London: Bell, 1964.

Banister, Judith. *Old English Silver*. New York: Putnam, 1965.

Courtauld, S. A. *Some Silver Wrought by the Courtauld Family*. Oxford: Blackwell, 1940.

Defenbacher, D. S. *Knife/Fork/Spoon*. Minneapolis: Walker Art Center, 1951.

Ensko, S. G. G. and Wenham, E. G. *English Silver, 1675-1825*. New York: Ensko, 1937.

Hayden, Arthur. *Chats on Old Silver*. London: Unwin, 1915.

Hayward, J. E. *Huguenot Silver in England, 1688-1727*. London: Faber, 1959.

Howard, Montague. *Old English Silver*. London: Batsford, 1903.

Hughes, G. Bernard. *Small Antique Silverware*. London: Batsford, 1967.

Jackson, Sir Charles. *English Goldsmiths and Their Marks*. Second edition. London: Batsford, 1949.

Jones, Edward A. *Old Silver of Europe and America*. London: Batsford, 1928.

Oman, Charles C. *English Domestic Silver*. Fifth edition. London: A. & C. Black, 1962.

Penzer, N. M. *Paul Storr, the Last of the Goldsmiths*. London: Batsford, 1954.

Phillips, P. A. S. *Paul de Lamerie, His Life and Work*. London: Batsford, 1935.

Rupert, E. G. *Apostle Spoons*. London: Oxford, 1929.

Watts, Wilbur. *Old English Silver*. New York: Scribner, 1924.

Wenham, Edward. *Domestic Silver of Great Britain and Ireland*. London: Oxford, 1931.

Wyler, Seymour. *The Book of Old Silver*. New York: Crown, 1937.

# Index

## SIGMUND A. LAVINE

has two ambitions—to own a talking parrot and to spend all his time digging out little-known facts about people and animals. As yet he has not acquired the parrot, but he has devoted long hours to the search for colorful material to enliven his biographies and nature books.

Neither a parrot nor research interested him as a young man because he was determined to become an actor. This was only natural since his parents were members of John Craig's famous stock company. However, persuaded by stars, bit players, and stagehands to "get an education," he enrolled in Boston University's School of Journalism.

While in college he edited the campus humorous monthly, was feature editor of the weekly newspaper, played leads in Shakespeare productions, and stage-managed five annual presentations of the Gilbert and Sullivan Association. Out of this last-named activity came his hobby of collecting anything "by or about" the creators of *The Mikado*, *Pinafore*, and the other Savoy operettas.

Meanwhile, he became more and more active in newspaper work, both as a feature writer for the *Boston Sunday Post* and as sports correspondent for two wire services, but acting ambitions were not forgotten. Then came the Great Depression and, as there was no demand for either journalists or actors, he returned to the classroom.

After receiving his M.Ed., he taught in a United States Government Indian School at Belcourt, North Dakota, for two years, learned to speak both Sioux and Cree, and talk in sign language. He was invited to tribal dances, ceremonies, and Indian court in reservations throughout Canada and the Northwest.

Upon returning to Boston in 1934, he began teaching in the schools of that city and is now an assistant principal. As soon as he became accustomed to the feel of concrete rather than prairie under his feet, he began to transcribe the field notes he had accumulated while observing wildlife in North Dakota, and he continued his study of scientific literature dealing with the ways of animals. In time, out of this continuous research came nearly a dozen nature books. Meanwhile he was lecturing on Indian folklore and current books, writing natural history articles and literary criticism. He still engages in these activities and his work has appeared in national publications, while his column on books for young adults is a regular feature of the Boston *Herald*.

With his wife, their son Jerrold, and a whippet answering to the unlikely name of Morrisey—the latest of a long line of prize-winning dogs owned by the Lavines—he lives in a house filled with books, fish tanks, art glass, and historical china. For relaxation, his family attends country auctions, goes "antiquing," or browses in bookstores, but their greatest pleasure is truck gardening on a piece of rocky New Hampshire land.